# MEAL PREP LUNCHES

# MEAL PREP LUNCHES

80 Recipes for Ready-to-Go Meals

*Michelle Vodrazka*

PHOTOGRAPHY BY ANDREW PURCELL

**ROCKRIDGE
PRESS**

For general information on our other products and services or to obtain technical support, please contact our Customer Care Department within the United States at (866) 744-2665, or outside the United States at (510) 253-0500.

Rockridge Press publishes its books in a variety of electronic and print formats. Some content that appears in print may not be available in electronic books, and vice versa.

TRADEMARKS: Rockridge Press and the Rockridge Press logo are trademarks or registered trademarks of Callisto Media Inc. and/or its affiliates, in the United States and other countries, and may not be used without written permission. All other trademarks are the property of their respective owners. Rockridge Press is not associated with any product or vendor mentioned in this book.

Interior and Cover Designer: Francesca Pacchini
Art Producer: Sue Bischofberger
Editor: Gurvinder Singh Gandu
Production Editor: Mia Moran
Photography © 2020 Andrew Purcell, front cover and all interior images; Darren Muir, back cover

ISBN: Print 978-1-64611-661-4
eBook 978-1-64611-662-1

R0

# CONTENTS

# INTRODUCTION

Hi there! I'm Michelle. I'm a former fitness competitor, mom of five, and author of *The Bodybuilding Meal Prep Cookbook*. As a busy professional and on-the-go mom, I love a good, nutritious, hassle-free lunch. My guess is that if you've picked up this book, you do, too. Throughout the next 10 weeks, I'll be your guide as you learn to prepare healthy, portable, and totally doable midday meals.

I'll be honest: When it comes to preparing a workday lunch, I've been through it all—from soggy salads and sandwiches to the soup spills that have disgraced my lunch box. But, by the same token, when I haven't made myself something sustaining to eat during the day, I've ended up regretting it. No one wants to sit through an afternoon meeting with hangry Michelle! In short, I realized that *what* I eat for lunch matters, and I've learned a lot from trial and error. Luckily, you get to benefit from my experience and avoid the mistakes I first made when I began my meal prep journey.

I've seen firsthand that, by implementing a few basic formulas, this process reaps major dividends. With just a little time pregaming in the kitchen, I'm able to set myself up for success with nutritious, grab-and-go meals that keep me filled throughout the week—and you can do the same.

After all, a balanced lunch isn't just nice to have in theory. Eating well in the middle of the day boosts mood, provides energy, maintains steady blood sugar, and keeps your appetite from getting out of control so you don't binge at dinner or overindulge at happy hour. But many of us don't get the lunches we want or really need.

While you may be fortunate enough to have a workplace cafeteria or be next door to endless fast food or restaurant chains, these institutions aren't easy on the wallet—nor are they usually the greatest purveyors of healthy, appetizing fare. Plus, they can "eat up" your lunch break pretty quickly. Especially for those in the nine-to-five grind, lunch may be the one time during your day that you get a break to reconnect with yourself and tune in to your body.

So I propose we both save you some time and cash, and bust that ham-and-cheese, same-old-salad or whatever-leftovers-I-can-rummage-up rut and reimagine that workweek lunch. As you make your way through this book, my hope is that you'll learn through experience that prepping your week's lunches isn't as daunting as it may seem.

Ten preset plans for weekly meals will guide you through more than two months of healthy midday eating. Plus, you'll find bonus lunch recipes for extra variety and snack recipes that are perfect for the workday. These bonus recipes can help you create lunches beyond the original 10 weeks. By the end, you'll have all the tools you need to continue the meal prep process on your own. Or, if you prefer, you can easily cycle back through the recipes provided.

Ready to actually feel excited to open your lunch box each day? Let's dive in!

# Part I

# THE MIDDAY MEAL, REIMAGINED

# Chapter 1
# MEAL PREP: IT'S WHAT'S FOR LUNCH!

You've probably heard that meal prep is the domain of only healthy food bloggers, calorie-counters, or bodybuilders. But I'm here to tell you it works for regular people looking for a simple answer to lunch, too! Setting aside a chunk of time at the beginning of the week (or, really, whenever works for you) allows you to face the workweek with far less stress.

Prepping your lunches takes the guesswork out of your lunch break. No more wondering how or where you're going to get a bite when you have only a brief window of time. No more grabbing whatever uninspiring leftovers your fridge coughs up at 7:00 a.m. and no more downing calorie-laden restaurant meals you didn't really want.

In fact, planning and prepping your lunches is a surefire way to feed yourself healthy, nutritious meals chosen by *you*, not a chef or catering queen. Plus, these homemade meals are guaranteed to save you tons of time and cost less than anything you'd pick up on the go. Now you have more time to watch Netflix, socialize, chill with your family, cuddle with your dog, or do some housework (ick).

# PERKS OF THE PREP

Let's explore a little more about why prepping your lunches is totally worth the effort.

## EAT HEALTHIER

When you choose your own ingredients for lunch and you make your meals from scratch, you put yourself in control of your own health. The recipes in this book will provide you with colorful and vibrant foods that you'll not only be excited to eat, but that will nourish your body with a plethora of nutrients.

## SAVE TIME

I won't lie: When prepping an entire week's worth of lunches in one shot, you'll have to set aside a dedicated chunk of time in the kitchen. But guess what? After that, it's smooth sailing! I've provided an easy-to-follow template for maximum efficiency each week. This way, you'll get more time with the people you love, doing the things you enjoy—and, of course, you'll also be enjoying the food itself.

## SAVE MONEY

When it comes to feeding ourselves and our families, most of us want to stay within a budget. Prepping your lunches is a great way to minimize cost, leaving room for the occasional pizza night or dinner out. Any time you make a meal at home, you're likely to spend less than when you eat out. This book's formula also uses certain "star" ingredients in unique ways each week to keep costs down and prevent you from purchasing specialized items you'll only use once.

## REDUCE STRESS

No one relishes the craziness of a busy morning trying to bundle kids off to school or rush to work. And let's be real: deciding what to make for lunch amid all the chaos is exhausting. Meal prep takes that element of stress off your proverbial plate. Plus, it provides you with built-in portion control, helps balance your midday mood, and makes the question of what you should eat for lunch today obsolete.

## GET ORGANIZED

Imagine cleaning fewer dishes, purchasing and storing fewer ingredients, and actually enjoying your time in the kitchen. Ready to opt in to all these organizational benefits? Then let's get going.

# THE ANATOMY OF A BALANCED LUNCH

Despite what you may remember from the multilayered Food Pyramid of days gone by, building a balanced meal doesn't actually have to be complicated. In fact, I'm happy to break it down into just three categories: protein, fiber, and fat.

**PROTEIN** builds muscle, heals wounds, and creates important hormones and enzymes in the body. You're probably familiar with many sources of protein, such as meat, fish, eggs, dairy, beans, and soy foods. The recipes in this book will provide you with a mix of animal- and plant-based protein.

**FIBER** is the part of a plant your body can't process, which is why it's so good for digestion. Getting enough fiber is associated with reduced risk of a number of diseases, regulating blood sugar, and maintaining a healthy weight. In these recipes, you'll take in plenty of it from whole grains, legumes, nuts, seeds, vegetables, and fruits.

**FAT** isn't the enemy! Your body needs it for a number of biological processes, like nutrient absorption, hormone production, and energy production. Plus, it makes food taste better. Fatty fish, avocados, olives, nuts, seeds, certain oils, and dairy are all healthy sources. You'll find them in the recipes that follow.

# KEYS TO MEAL PREP SUCCESS

If you're new to meal prep, there are some key steps I recommend for getting things started. These tips are sure to make your life easier.

## CHOOSE A DEDICATED PREP DAY

Unless your schedule varies wildly from week to week, it's typically best to choose one particular day for prep and stick with it. This way you know when to shop and plan, and when to block off a bit of time in your calendar. Committing to a certain day also makes you more likely to stick with the program. Prioritize this time as a good-for-you activity that's part of your self-care—and schedule other commitments around it.

## MAKE A CONTAINER INVESTMENT

Okay, it may sound weird to "invest" in a stock of food containers, but stick with me on this. Getting the right containers is totally worthwhile for several reasons. Certain containers are better than others for holding warm foods, storing meals in an organized fashion, and preventing spills and soggy lunches. Plus, purchasing a set of meal prep containers can be fun and motivating! We'll talk more about exactly which containers are best for meal prep in To-Go Storage (page 15).

## START WITH AN ORGANIZED SPACE

Before anyone jumps into meal prep, I always encourage them to start with a clean slate. Wash and put away any dishes in the sink, get your containers ready, and check your list twice and verify that you have all the ingredients on hand. Most important, make sure you're in the right frame of mind. That might mean sending the kids out for a "playdate" with your spouse, playing your favorite music, or turning on the game or your favorite TV show.

## MULTITASK

I promise you'll get better at this as you go, but the beauty of making all your meals in one concentrated burst is that multiple kitchen appliances can work at once, saving you time. Multitasking is the key to getting your meal prep done in a reasonable amount of time. Throughout this book, I'll offer tips for doing several things at once, like chopping, baking, steaming, sautéing, and slow cooking. Pretty soon, you'll find that your kitchen is a well-oiled machine!

### REMEMBER YOUR GOALS

Without a doubt, there may come a day when you feel like you'd rather run out for a burger than prep your lunch. And maybe occasionally you do—no biggie. But for the long haul, try to keep your goals in the forefront of your mind. What prompted you to prep your lunches? Was it convenience? Your health? Your wallet? Your appearance? Be honest, because it can help you stay the course!

# COMMON MEAL PREP MISTAKES (AND HOW TO AVOID THEM)

It can take quite a bit of trial and error to figure out a meal prep routine that works for you and your family. To save you some time, I've compiled some key tips to help you avoid the most common meal prep mistakes.

### OVERCOMPLICATING THE RECIPES

The point of meal prep is simplicity. But all too often (especially when starting out) we tend to make the process and the meals themselves more complex than they need to be. In this book, I promise I won't burn you out on overcomplicated recipes or attempts to do too much at once.

### OVERSIMPLIFYING THE RECIPES

Just like it's possible to make things too complicated when meal prepping, it's also common to make them too simple—aka boring. Your lunches need variety! Keeping things interesting in your lunch box helps you stay on track with meal prep and all its benefits.

### USING THE WRONG TYPE OF CONTAINER

Not all containers are created equal. As we discussed, it's extremely helpful to invest in a variety of storage containers that work better for different-size portions, help keep your foods separated, and that are more compatible with hot or cold foods.

### CHOOSING CONVENIENCE OVER HEALTH

When convenience is your goal, it's way too easy to focus on fixing meals quickly instead of making them nutritious. You'll find the recipes provided here serve both purposes.

## PREPPING TOO FAR AHEAD

In a perfect world, all foods would keep in the fridge or freezer indefinitely. But in reality, certain foods just won't last beyond a few days—we're looking at you, leafy lettuce salad. Cooking your meals too far in advance can leave you with soggy, unappetizing options later in the week. Throughout the next 10 weeks, I'll guide you through the process of timing your cooking *just right*, to maximize flavor and freshness.

## TIME-SAVING SHOPPING TIPS

One of the most appealing things about meal prep is that it saves you time. Here's how to make sure you keep time spent shopping to a minimum.

**KEEP A RUNNING GROCERY LIST:** This is rule number one for saving time and stress and avoiding last-minute emergency grocery runs. In addition to the weekly lists provided here, keep a running tally on the contents of your fridge and pantry, adding staple items when they get low.

**BUY IN BULK WHEN IT MAKES SENSE:** When ingredients that you use frequently go on sale, stock up on extras. Store surplus in the pantry or the freezer, if possible, but make sure you review what's stored regularly so you don't end up with freezer-burned chicken, rancid nuts, or expired sauces.

**LEAVE THE KIDS AT HOME:** We love you, kids, but you sure make shopping stressful. When possible, find a way to leave little ones at home so that you can focus on getting what you actually need—not barbecue chips or sugary cereal.

**SHOP DURING OFF-PEAK HOURS:** If you really want to save time at the grocery store, don't join the masses on Saturday or Sunday morning. Instead, try avoiding crowds and long lines by doing your shopping during off-hours or during the workweek.

**PARK NEAR THE SHOPPING CART RECEPTACLE:** I learned this one from my husband, and it's such a lifesaver. Parking right next to the grocery cart receptacle kills two birds with one stone—returning your cart is easier, and it's simpler to remember where you parked!

# Chapter 2
# THE WELL-STOCKED KITCHEN

As you start your meal prep journey, it's important to note that part of preparation is readying your kitchen. In this chapter, we'll talk about how to stock your pantry and fridge with the best ingredients for streamlined lunch-making, plus take a look at what equipment and tools are best suited for prepping and storing your meals.

If this sounds like a lot of work, don't worry—you won't have to do a kitchen remodel. Most of the tools required are things you're likely to have on hand already. And don't fall for the myth that you need a giant space to make lunch prep successful. Even a small kitchen can serve as a multitasking meal prep workshop.

First, let's take a look at some of the best staple ingredients to have at the ready. Don't worry if you're new to cooking—once you get in the groove of choosing good-for-you ingredients, it'll quickly become second nature.

# PANTRY

When you open your pantry, what do you see? Are the building blocks of healthy lunches sitting there just waiting to be assembled? If not, maybe it's time to change things up. Here are some of the shelf-stable ingredients you'll want to have available.

## GRAINS, VEGETABLES, AND MORE

Filling and full of nutrients, grains, legumes, and vegetables serve as the base for tons of healthy meals. Some to keep handy include:

- Pasta
- Quinoa
- Couscous
- Rice
- Oats
- Sweet potatoes
- Regular potatoes
- Squash
- Onions
- Fresh garlic
- Canned beans
- Canned tomatoes
- Chicken or vegetable stock

## NUTS AND SEEDS

They may be small, but nuts and seeds pack a mighty punch of protein and healthy fats. Stock up on the following:

- Almonds
- Cashews
- Pecans
- Walnuts
- Pine nuts
- Hemp seeds
- Flaxseed meal
- Pumpkin seeds
- Nut and seed butters

## OILS, VINEGARS, AND MORE

To make tasty sauces for drizzling and dipping, it's great to have an arsenal of oils, vinegars, and other dressings such as:

- Olive oil
- Grapeseed oil
- Canola oil
- Balsamic vinegar
- Apple cider vinegar
- Red wine vinegar
- Soy sauce

## SEASONINGS AND SPICES

Herbs and spices add interest to just about any dish and have virtually zero calories. Some good choices include:

- Dried basil
- Dried oregano
- Dried cumin
- Chili powder
- Curry powder
- Cinnamon
- Onion powder
- Garlic powder
- Paprika
- Dried rosemary
- Dried thyme
- Dried Italian seasoning
- Red pepper flakes
- Sea salt
- Freshly ground black pepper

## REFRIGERATOR

Now that we've tackled your pantry, let's make your refrigerator meal prep friendly. Choosing nutrient-dense ingredients that won't expire quickly paves the way for healthy, easy cooking. You'll be given a shopping list for each week's meals, but it's also a good idea to keep your refrigerator stocked with go-to items such as:

- Cow's milk or a nondairy milk of your choice
- Unsweetened or vanilla Greek yogurt
- Cheese: bar cheese and crumbles
- Eggs
- Fresh fruit, such as grapes, strawberries, blueberries, raspberries, blackberries, apples, oranges, pears, and melons
- Fresh veggies, such as carrots, broccoli, zucchini, peppers, cauliflower, celery, and asparagus
- Leafy greens
- Fresh herbs like rosemary, thyme, parsley, cilantro, and basil
- Fresh meat, including chicken breasts and/or thighs, steak, ground beef or turkey, lamb, pork tenderloin or chops, and sausages
- Fresh fish like salmon, tuna, mackerel, tilapia, or cod

## EQUIPMENT

I won't burden you with outfitting your kitchen with a ton of wacky gadgets just to meal prep your lunches. Most of what you'll be making will require only standard kitchen equipment, such as:

- Oven and range
- Microwave
- Slow cooker
- Roasting and baking pans
- Pots of various sizes, with lids
- Pans of various sizes, with lids
- Mixing bowls of various sizes
- Blender or food processor
- Mixer
- Cutting board
- Paring knife and chef's knife
- Whisk
- Measuring cups and spoons
- Potato masher
- Spatula
- Grater
- Peeler
- Meat thermometer
- Silicone brush

13

## CONDIMENTS TO SPRUCE THINGS UP

When a meal needs that little something extra, it's worthwhile to have some flavor-boosting condiments on hand. Here are a few to keep around the house (or even at your desk or work refrigerator):

- Sriracha or other hot sauce
- Olive oil or balsamic vinegar
- Ketchup
- Barbecue sauce
- Honey or maple syrup
- Soy sauce or tamari
- Mustard: Dijon, yellow, or stone-ground
- Mayonnaise
- Pesto
- Salsa
- Hummus
- Tahini
- Spice blends or seasonings
- Cinnamon
- Lemon or lime juice
- Sea salt and pepper

## DESK LUNCH SNACKS

There's a better way to nourish your body than overly processed snacks. Choosing good-for-you things to nibble on throughout the workday fuels your body and mind far better than convenience straight out of a package or a box. Here are some healthy options to keep on hand:

- Popcorn
- Fresh or dried fruit
- Hummus
- Chips and salsa
- Nuts and nut butters
- Whole-grain crackers
- Cheese
- Cottage cheese or yogurt
- Oatmeal-based bowls or overnight oats
- Homemade energy balls or granola bars
- Beef jerky
- Roasted chickpeas

# TO-GO STORAGE

As I've mentioned previously, effective, convenient meal prep is all about containers. You'll be putting some considerable time and energy into your lunch prep journey, so you want to be sure the vessels that hold your food are also keeping up their end of the deal. When making an entire week's worth of lunches, it's vital that containers can hold various types and portions of food, won't leak, and can stack neatly to fit in your fridge and lunch box. It's also helpful for visual appeal if you find them attractive. Now, go and throw out that stained, old, cracked Tupperware.

## TYPES OF CONTAINERS

Let's get down to the nitty-gritty. Which meal prep containers should you actually purchase? If you've already started shopping, you've probably noticed that there are innumerable options to choose from. The decision is yours, of course, but here's a look at pros and cons of some more popular options.

### GLASS
It's the classic type you see in so many Insta-worthy meal prep photos: the clean, crisp, transparent glass food container. Glass containers get positive attention for good reason. They're dishwasher-, freezer-, and microwave-safe, and their see-through nature shows off the tasty food they hold inside. There are tons of different options, including mason jars, which are great for stackable and liquid meals. The two downsides: they're heavy and fragile.

### STAINLESS STEEL
Sleek and sophisticated, stainless steel containers make an attractive collection in your fridge or pantry. In general, they also tend to do well in the freezer and dishwasher. Many people prefer them over plastic, since they won't leach any questionable chemicals into your food. But stainless steel is not microwave-safe, and it can be heavy as well.

### REUSABLE PLASTIC
Reusable plastic containers are the "old reliable" of the food-storage world. They can typically go in the dishwasher, fridge, and freezer without issue. On the other hand, they stain easily and don't keep food as fresh as long as glass containers do. Furthermore, some people have concerns about the chemicals they may transfer to food, especially when heated. If you are unsure of the quality of the plastic container, it's best to opt for a different

material. If plastic is your preference, look for BPA-free versions.

## LUNCH BOXES

Don't forget to pick up an insulated lunch box or bag. Make sure it's big enough to fit your preferred style of container, along with some ice packs to keep your food stored safely. I find that the 12-can cooler bags tend to work really well.

# FOOD STORAGE GUIDELINES

With all the hard work you'll be putting in on prepping crave-worthy lunches, the last thing you want is for them to go bad before you can eat them. Storing food safely is critical, so let's take a moment to review best practices.

## PORTIONING/PACKING

Before storing hot foods in a cold place, be sure to let them cool slightly and always leave a little "headspace" in your containers, since foods can expand or contract depending on temperature.

## PROPER LABELING

We all think we'll remember exactly when we stored that lasagna or casserole, but days sometimes whiz by and blend into each other and the date they were prepared gets harder and harder to recall. So just purchase a roll of cling stickers and label your meals with the date you made them.

## THAWING/REHEATING

When lunchtime rolls around and you're ready to enjoy the fruits of your labor, you may need (or want) to reheat your meal. Simply reheat in a microwave-safe container at 30-second intervals until heated to your liking.

## MAINTAINING HOT OR COLD TEMPS

Don't have a fridge at work? Pick up a few ice packs and an insulated lunch bag to keep your lunch safely chilled. Likewise, if your workplace doesn't have a microwave, you may want to invest in a thermos or insulated lunch box.

Here's how long common foods last in the fridge:

| FOOD | FRIDGE |
|---|---|
| Salads: egg salad, tuna salad, chicken salad, pasta salad | 3 TO 5 DAYS |
| Ground meat | 1 TO 2 DAYS |
| Steaks: beef, pork, lamb (raw) | 3 TO 5 DAYS |
| Chops: beef, lamp, pork (raw) | 3 TO 5 DAYS |
| Roasts: beef, pork, lamb (raw) | 3 TO 5 DAYS |
| Whole chicken or turkey | 1 TO 2 DAYS |
| Pieces: chicken or turkey (raw) | 1 TO 2 DAYS |
| Soups and stews with vegetables and meat | 3 TO 4 DAYS |
| Pizza | 3 TO 4 DAYS |
| Beef, lamb, pork, or chicken (cooked) | 3 TO 4 DAYS |

# WHAT TO EXPECT FROM MEAL PREPS AND RECIPES

We've covered a lot of ground already! I hope these first couple of chapters have given you a solid understanding of the benefits you can expect by meal prepping your lunches, from saving money to reducing stress, to giving you more time to do other things you enjoy. Now it's time to put it all into practice.

In the 10-week plan that follows, you'll be given two recipes per week. Step-by-step instructions will walk you through the process of what to make and when, as well as the best way to store your lunches. Each recipe comes complete with nutrition info. Plus, I've noted where there are dairy-free, gluten-free, nut-free, vegetarian, or vegan meals. I want you to know exactly what you're getting and feel confident that it's good for you!

You'll also find that each week's plan focuses around a handful of repeat ingredients used in creative ways, making less work for you. We'll explore a gamut of recipes that will include lighter fare, like grain bowls, salads, and pasta dishes, as well as more substantial foods such as pot roast, fajitas, and baked salmon.

Each week features one vegetarian recipe and one meat-based recipe. Feel free to make them as is or to adapt them to your personal dietary needs if needed. (There are instructions on how to do so in the shopping lists, as well as on each individual recipe page.)

Each meal provides the critical building blocks we discussed previously: protein, fiber, and fat. Finally, you'll have the chance to mix and match your own meals with a list of additional recipe chapters for main dishes, snacks, and condiments. With these vibrant, flavorful recipes, I think you'll look forward to each new week of cooking and eating.

So, what's for lunch? Let's find out!

White Bean and Zoodle Zuppa

Page 24

## Chapter 3
# WEEK 1

The star ingredients this week are ground turkey and zucchini. Zucchini is an extremely versatile ingredient that's easy to prepare, and it blends well with a variety of flavors. You can also substitute any summer squash for the zucchini, depending on what's available, such as pattypan squash or yellow squash. Ground turkey is an excellent lean source of protein, but feel free to substitute ground chicken or lean ground beef for the turkey. Each recipe can be adapted to fit your personal dietary preferences, whether it's meat-based or vegetarian/vegan. If desired, simply add the optional meat-based protein to a vegetarian dish or vice versa.

22

# YOUR LUNCHES THIS WEEK

| DAY | LUNCH |
| --- | --- |
| MONDAY | **White Bean and Zoodle Zuppa** |
| TUESDAY | **Turkey Zoodle Skillet** |
| WEDNESDAY | **White Bean and Zoodle Zuppa** |
| THURSDAY | **Turkey Zoodle Skillet** |
| FRIDAY | **White Bean and Zoodle Zuppa** |

# STEP-BY-STEP PREP

1.  Peel and chop onion, bell peppers, and carrot and set aside.

2.  Use a vegetable peeler to peel the zucchini into long, flat ribbons.

3.  Brown the ground turkey in a skillet, breaking it up with a wooden spoon as you do. If adding ground turkey to the soup recipe, split it into two even batches. (If making lunches all vegetarian, omit this step.)

4.  Open all canned items and drain the beans. Leave the tomatoes undrained.

5.  Prepare the White Bean and Zoodle Zuppa (page 24) in a large pot as directed, using half of the onion, half of the bell pepper, half of the zucchini, and the carrot.

6.  Prepare the Turkey Zoodle Skillet (page 25) in a large skillet as directed using the remaining half of the onion, half of the bell pepper, and half of the zucchini.

7.  Portion the White Bean and Zoodle Zuppa evenly into three single-serving containers. Refrigerate the containers.

8.  Portion the Turkey Zoodle Skillet into two single-serving containers (half of the recipe in each container). Refrigerate the containers.

# WHITE BEAN AND ZOODLE ZUPPA

**DAIRY-FREE, GLUTEN-FREE, NUT-FREE, VEGAN**

*Servings: 3 / Prep time: 10 minutes / Cook time: 15 minutes*

Soup (*zuppa* in Italian) is a great meal prep food, and this one is loaded with savory Italian flavors, along with hearty white beans and nutrition-packed veggies. Carrying it in a thermos will keep the soup nice and warm until you're ready to enjoy it, and prep is super easy. Soup also freezes well, so you can always double or triple your batch and store it in single servings in the freezer for up to one year. If frozen, reheat on the stove top.

2 tablespoons olive oil

½ yellow onion, chopped

½ red bell pepper, stem, ribs, and seeds removed, chopped

1 carrot, chopped

1 (14.5-ounce) can low-sodium vegetable broth

1 (15-ounce) can crushed tomatoes, undrained

1 (15-ounce) can cannellini beans (white beans), drained

1 tablespoon dried Italian seasoning

1 teaspoon garlic powder

½ teaspoon sea salt

⅛ teaspoon freshly cracked black pepper

Pinch red pepper flakes (optional)

2 medium zucchini, cut into "ribbons" using a vegetable peeler

1. In a large pot, heat the olive oil over medium-high heat until it shimmers.

2. Add the onion, bell pepper, and carrot and cook, stirring occasionally, until the vegetables soften, about 5 minutes.

3. Add the vegetable broth, crushed tomatoes with their juices, cannellini beans, Italian seasoning, garlic powder, salt, pepper, and red pepper flakes, if using. Bring to a simmer and reduce the heat to medium-low. Simmer on low, stirring occasionally, for 10 minutes.

4. Add the zucchini. Simmer, stirring occasionally, for 5 minutes more.

5. Split evenly into three single-serving containers and refrigerate.

> **DIETARY SWAP:** If you'd like to include a meat-based protein, you can add 10 ounces of cooked ground turkey in step 5 when you add the zucchini.

Per Serving: Calories: 305; Total Fat: 11g; Saturated Fat: 1.5g; Cholesterol: 0mg; Carbohydrates: 42g; Fiber: 12g; Protein: 12g

# TURKEY ZOODLE SKILLET

DAIRY-FREE, GLUTEN-FREE, NUT-FREE

*Servings: 2 / Prep time: 10 minutes / Cook time: 10 minutes*

This simple skillet is easy to make—and easy to customize to your own tastes. Feel free to substitute seasonal veggies, replace the turkey with ground chicken or lean ground beef, or add the herbs and spices you have available to change the flavor. If you prefer not to cut the zucchini into ribbons to look like pasta ribbons, you can also simply chop them into ½-inch-thick pieces with a paring knife.

2 tablespoons olive oil

½ yellow onion, chopped

½ red bell pepper, stem, ribs, and seeds removed, chopped

1 (10-ounce) can chopped tomatoes, undrained

½ teaspoon chili powder

½ teaspoon ground cumin

½ teaspoon garlic powder

½ teaspoon sea salt

10 ounces ground turkey, cooked

2 zucchini, cut into pasta ribbons with a vegetable peeler

1. In a large skillet, heat the olive oil over medium-high heat until it shimmers.

2. Add the onion and bell pepper. Cook, stirring occasionally, until the vegetables soften, about 5 minutes.

3. Add the tomatoes, chili powder, cumin, garlic powder, and salt. Bring to a simmer. Add the cooked ground turkey and zucchini. Cook, stirring, for 5 minutes.

4. Split evenly into two single-serving containers and refrigerate.

**DIETARY SWAP:** Make this vegetarian by replacing the ground turkey with a 14-ounce can of drained kidney beans.

Per Serving: Calories: 372; Total Fat: 24g; Saturated Fat: 4.5g; Cholesterol: 95mg; Carbohydrates: 9g; Fiber: 2.5g; Protein: 30g

25

Orange-Sriracha Chicken Thighs
with Rice and Veggies
*Page 31*

*Chapter 4*
# WEEK 2

**BROCCOLI AND EDAMAME STIR-FRY** 30

**ORANGE-SRIRACHA CHICKEN THIGHS WITH RICE AND VEGGIES** 31

Legumes and broccoli take center stage this week, and with good reason. Legumes are a great source of vegetable protein, they keep well, they're inexpensive, and they don't require a lot of extra work to prepare. It's also easy to substitute one legume for another, which gives you lots of variations on these two simple prep recipes. Likewise, broccoli is a powerhouse food that packs a nutritional punch. As in the previous chapter, each recipe has an option to either add animal protein or subtract it, depending on whether or not you're vegetarian, so it's super easy to adapt these recipes to meet your own dietary needs.

## YOUR LUNCHES THIS WEEK

| DAY | LUNCH |
|---|---|
| MONDAY | **Broccoli and Edamame Stir-Fry** |
| TUESDAY | **Orange-Sriracha Chicken Thighs with Rice and Veggies** |
| WEDNESDAY | **Broccoli and Edamame Stir-Fry** |
| THURSDAY | **Orange-Sriracha Chicken Thighs with Rice and Veggies** |
| FRIDAY | **Broccoli and Edamame Stir-Fry** |

# STEP-BY-STEP PREP

1. If cooking the brown rice, combine 1 cup of rice and 1¼ cups water in a pot. Heat over high and bring to a boil. Reduce the temperature to low and cover. Cook according to package directions until tender. Remove from the heat and fluff with a fork. Portion into ½-cup serving sizes.

2. While the rice cooks, prepare your chicken, broccoli, and beans as directed below.

3. Pat chicken thighs with paper towels and cut into 1-inch pieces. (Omit this step if making vegetarian.)*

4. Preheat your oven to 425°F.

5. Rinse the vegetables in a colander. Drain.

6. Chop the vegetables and set them aside.

7. If making this all vegetarian, pat the tofu dry with paper towels and cut it into one-inch pieces.* (Omit this step if swapping in chicken instead.)

8. Zest one orange with a rasp-style grater (you need about 1 teaspoon grated zest). Juice two oranges and set the liquid aside (about ½ cup orange juice). Juice the lime and set the liquid aside (about 2 tablespoons lime juice).

9. Whisk together the sauce for the chicken or tofu.

10. In a large bowl, toss 2 cups of broccoli with the green beans, shallots, and chicken thighs (or tofu) with the sauce and place on the sheet pan. Put the pan in the oven for 45 minutes.

11. While the thighs and vegetables roast, prepare the Broccoli and Edamame Stir-Fry (page 30).

12. Cook the vegetables in a skillet or wok as directed.

13. Whisk together the sauce for the Broccoli and Edamame Stir-Fry (page 30).

14. Add the sauce to the stir-fry.

15. Remove the chicken and broccoli from the oven when done.

16. Assemble lunches as indicated in each recipe.

# BROCCOLI AND EDAMAME STIR-FRY

DAIRY-FREE, NUT-FREE, VEGAN

*Servings: 3 / Prep time: 10 minutes / Cook time: 10 minutes*

Edamame, or soybeans, are a great source of vegetarian protein, and they add a nice, crisp-tender texture to all kinds of vegetarian stir-fries. Cut your broccoli into small florets so they cook nice and quickly, and you'll have this simple lunch put together in 20 minutes or less. Reheat in the microwave or serve chilled.

2 tablespoons olive oil

1 bunch scallions, chopped

3 cups broccoli florets

2 cups fresh or frozen shelled edamame

1 tablespoon soy sauce

½ teaspoon sriracha

½ teaspoon garlic powder

½ teaspoon ground ginger

Juice of 1 lime

1 teaspoon cornstarch

1½ cups cooked brown rice

1. In a large pot, skillet, or wok, heat the olive oil over medium-high heat until it shimmers.

2. Add the scallions, broccoli, and edamame. Cook, stirring occasionally, until the vegetables are crisp-tender, about 5 minutes.

3. In a small bowl, whisk together the soy sauce, sriracha, garlic powder, ground ginger, lime juice, and cornstarch. Add to the skillet. Cook, stirring, until the sauce thickens, 1 to 2 minutes. Let cool.

4. Portion ½ cup of the cooked brown rice into three containers, then top each with an equal portion of the stir-fry.

> **DIETARY SWAP:** If you'd like to make this non-vegetarian, remove the skin and bones from two raw chicken thighs and cut into one-inch pieces. Cook on medium-high heat in the olive oil before step 2 until browned and remove from the oil, setting the meat aside on a platter tented with foil to keep warm. Return to the pan after step 2 and before you add the sauce in step 3.

Per Serving: Calories: 388; Total Fat: 14g; Saturated Fat: 1.5g; Cholesterol: 0mg; Carbohydrates: 48g; Fiber: 9.5g; Protein: 18g

# ORANGE-SRIRACHA CHICKEN THIGHS WITH RICE AND VEGGIES

DAIRY-FREE, NUT-FREE

*Servings:* 2 / *Prep time:* 10 minutes / *Cook time:* 45 minutes

Roasting brings out the deep flavors in the broccoli and caramelizes the orange-sriracha sauce on the chicken thighs. While it takes a while for the thighs and broccoli to cook, it's hands-off time you can be using to do other things. You can adjust the spice level by adding more or less sriracha and save time by using precooked brown rice or save money by cooking your own.

Grated zest of 1 orange
(about 1 teaspoon)

Juice of 2 oranges
(about ½ cup)

1 tablespoon honey

1 teaspoon sriracha

½ teaspoon garlic powder

1 teaspoon soy sauce

1 tablespoon cornstarch

4 bone-in, skin-on chicken
thighs (4 to 6 ounces each)

2 cups broccoli florets

2 cups fresh green
beans, halved

6 shallots, peeled and
quartered lengthwise

1 cup cooked brown rice

1. Preheat your oven to 425°F.

2. In a large bowl, whisk together the orange zest, orange juice, honey, sriracha, garlic powder, soy sauce, and cornstarch.

3. Add the chicken thighs, broccoli, green beans, and shallots and toss to coat with the sauce.

4. Place the coated mixture in a single layer on a sheet pan.

5. Bake in the preheated oven until the thighs reach an internal temperature of 165°F, about 45 minutes. Remove from oven and let cool.

6. Divide into two portions with 2 thighs each and an equal amounts of broccoli, beans, shallots, and sauce for each.

7. Spoon ½ cup of rice each into two containers. Spoon the broccoli, beans, and sauce over the top. Add the chicken.

> **DIETARY SWAP:** Make this vegetarian by replacing the chicken thighs with 12 ounces of extra-firm tofu, cut into one-inch cubes. Add the tofu in place of the thighs in step 3.

Per Serving: Calories: 680; Total Fat: 26g; Saturated Fat: 7g; Cholesterol: 216mg; Carbohydrates: 66g; Fiber: 10g; Protein: 48g

Chickpea Buddha Bowls

*Page 37*

*Chapter 5*
# WEEK 3

## CHICKPEA BUDDHA BOWLS 37
## CHICKEN, HUMMUS, AND VEGGIE PITAS 38

This week's featured ingredients are chickpeas and roasted red bell pepper. You can easily roast your own red bell pepper, or you can buy it in jars in the canned vegetable aisle at the local grocer. If you do roast your own bell peppers, store them tightly sealed in the fridge for up to 2 weeks, or you can make a large batch and freeze them, tightly sealed, for up to 6 months. For chickpeas, your fastest route is to buy them in cans. But you can also cook large batches of chickpeas and store them in the fridge for up to 6 days or in the freezer in ½-cup serving sizes for up to 1 month.

## SHOPPING LIST

The shopping list below is for the two recipes as written. Substitutions for making both recipes either vegetarian or meat-based are as follows:

* If adding meat to Chickpea Buddha Bowls, increase quantity of chicken to 20 ounces.
* If making Chicken, Hummus, and Veggie Pitas vegetarian, skip chicken and get 9 ounces of tempeh instead.

### PRODUCE
☐ Avocado: 1 (optional)
☐ Bell pepper, red: 3
☐ Cabbage: 1 head (or coleslaw mix, 1 10-ounce bag)
☐ Carrot: 1
☐ Cilantro: 1 bunch
☐ Cucumber: 1
☐ Garlic: 1 bulb
☐ Lemon: 1
☐ Lime: 1
☐ Scallions: 1 bunch

### POULTRY
☐ Chicken breast, boneless, skinless: 12 ounces

### CANNED
☐ Artichoke hearts, marinated: 1 (9-ounce) jar
☐ Chickpeas, canned: 2 (14-ounce) cans
☐ Tahini: 1 jar (pantry item)

### GRAINS
☐ Rice, brown: 1 cup cooked or ½ cup uncooked

### OTHER
☐ Peanuts or cashews: ½ cup (about 2.5 ounces)
☐ Pita bread: 1 package (3 pitas)

## YOUR LUNCHES THIS WEEK

| DAY | LUNCH |
|---|---|
| MONDAY | **Chicken, Hummus, and Veggie Pitas** |
| TUESDAY | **Chickpea Buddha Bowls** |
| WEDNESDAY | **Chicken, Hummus, and Veggie Pitas** |
| THURSDAY | **Chickpea Buddha Bowls** |
| FRIDAY | **Chicken, Hummus, and Veggie Pitas** |

# STEP-BY-STEP PREP

1. If cooking the brown rice, combine ½ cup of rice and 1 cup water in a pot. Place on high and bring to a boil. Reduce the temperature to low and cover. Cook according to package directions until tender. Remove from heat and fluff with a fork. Portion into ½-cup serving sizes.

2. To roast your bell peppers, halve the peppers lengthwise and remove the stem, seeds, and ribs. Preheat your oven to 400°F. Brush the peppers on both sides with a small amount of olive oil and place on a rimmed baking sheet. Roast in the preheated oven for 15 minutes. Turn the peppers over and roast an additional 15 to 20 minutes, until soft. Cool completely.

3. Cook your chicken breasts. Put the chicken breasts on a rimmed baking sheet and sprinkle with a little sea salt and freshly cracked black pepper. Bake in the preheated oven until the chicken reaches an internal temperature of 165°F, about 25 minutes (flipping after 10 minutes). Cool and cut into pieces or shred with a fork.

4. Make the hummus according to the recipe instructions (page 38), or use store-bought hummus.

5. Make the Cilantro-Lime Dressing (page 150) and store in two small containers in the fridge. Shake before using.

6. Chop or shred the cabbage and set aside (or use about 2 cups of store-bought coleslaw mix). Chop the scallions and set aside. Grate the carrot and slice the cucumber.

7. Chop the peanuts (or cashews) and halve the pitas.

8. Drain and halve the artichoke hearts.

9. Assemble the Buddha bowls per the instructions (page 37) and refrigerate.

10. Assemble the pitas and refrigerate.

# CHICKPEA BUDDHA BOWLS

DAIRY-FREE, GLUTEN-FREE, VEGAN

*Servings: 2 / Prep time: 10 minutes*

This vegetarian meal can be as simple or as complex as you wish. Add more texture by adding half of a sliced avocado to your Buddha bowl, but slice the avocado and add it just before you consume, as avocado browns easily once it's exposed to oxygen. Store the other half in a zipper bag with the pit in it to keep it fresh longer. If you want more flavor in your brown rice, you can cook it with vegetable stock instead of water to add flavor, but it isn't necessary to do so.

1 cup cooked brown rice, cooled

1 (15-ounce) can chickpeas, drained

2 cups shredded cabbage

½ bunch scallions, chopped

1 carrot, grated

1 red bell pepper, stem, ribs, and seeds removed, sliced and roasted

½ cup chopped peanuts or cashews (omit for nut-free or replace with ½ cup pepitas)

1 cucumber, thinly sliced

Cilantro-Lime Dressing (page 150)

½ avocado, peeled and sliced (optional)

1. Mix the brown rice, chickpeas, cabbage, scallions, and carrot together.

2. Divide evenly into two containers.

3. Top each with equal amounts of the roasted red bell pepper, peanuts, and cucumber. Refrigerate.

4. Just before eating, top with half of the Cilantro-Lime Dressing (and avocado, if using) and toss to mix.

> **DIETARY SWAP:** To make this nonvegetarian, add 8 to 10 ounces of cooked chicken breast, chopped, to the bowls as you assemble them or save time by purchasing a precooked rotisserie chicken and adding chopped skinless chicken to the bowl.

Per Serving: Calories: 716; Total Fat: 37g; Saturated Fat: 5.5g; Cholesterol: 0mg; Carbohydrates: 78g; Fiber: 19g; Protein: 25g

# CHICKEN, HUMMUS, AND VEGGIE PITAS

DAIRY-FREE, NUT-FREE

*Servings: 3 / Prep time: 10 minutes*

It's easy to make your own hummus from canned chickpeas and tahini, or you can save time by purchasing premade hummus. It's the perfect condiment for these tasty pita sandwiches, but you can also use it as a quick dip for veggies or crackers. If you opt for store-bought hummus, then skip the first part of this recipe.

## For the hummus

1 (15-ounce) can chickpeas, drained

2 garlic cloves, minced

1 tablespoon tahini

Juice of 1 lemon

2 tablespoons olive oil

½ teaspoon sea salt

## For the pitas

12 ounces boneless, skinless chicken breasts, cooked and shredded

1 (9-ounce) jar marinated artichoke hearts, drained and halved

¾ cup grated cabbage

½ bunch scallions, chopped (about ½ cup)

2 red bell peppers, stem, ribs, and seeds removed, chopped and roasted

3 whole-wheat pitas, halved lengthwise

## To make the hummus

1. In a food processor or blender, combine the chickpeas, garlic, tahini, lemon juice, olive oil, and salt. Blend until smooth.

2. Store in three containers in the fridge.

## To make the pitas

3. In a bowl, combine the chicken, artichoke hearts, cabbage, scallions, and red bell peppers. Store in three zipper bags or containers.

4. Store the pitas in three individual zipper bags.

5. When ready to eat, spread the inside of each pita half with ⅙ of the hummus (about 2 tablespoons).

6. Add a third of the chicken breast, red bell peppers, cabbage, scallions, and artichoke hearts filling to a pita. Repeat the process for each day.

> **DIETARY SWAP:** Make this vegetarian by replacing the chicken breast with 9 ounces of chopped tempeh.

Per Serving: Calories: 641; Total Fat: 29g; Saturated Fat: 5g; Cholesterol: 63mg; Carbohydrates: 63g; Fiber: 18g; Protein: 38g

Crab and Mango–Stuffed Avocado
Page 45

## Chapter 6
# WEEK 4

This week we're spotlighting cooked quinoa and avocado. Avocado, once cut, browns quickly but you can slow down the browning process by adding acid (often in the form of citrus juice or vinegar) and storing it in an airtight container. In this case, you'll rub a lime or lemon wedge on the cut avocado or sprinkle it with lime or lemon juice and wrap it tightly in plastic. You can also wait and cut your avocado the day you plan to eat it to keep it at its freshest.

## SHOPPING LIST

The shopping list below is for the two recipes as written. Substitutions for making both recipes either vegetarian or meat-based are as follows:

* If adding meat to Quinoa and Veggie Bowls, get 3 (5-ounce) cans/pouches of salmon.
* If making Crab and Mango–Stuffed Avocados vegetarian, skip crab and get 1 (14-ounce) can hearts of palm.

### PRODUCE
☐ Avocado: 1
☐ Bell pepper, red: 1
☐ Brussels sprouts: 2 cups
☐ Chives: 1 bunch
☐ Dill: 1 bunch
☐ Garlic: 1 bulb
☐ Lemon: 1
☐ Limes: 1
☐ Mango: 1
☐ Onion, red: 2
☐ Parsley: 1 bunch
☐ Sweet potato: 1 medium

### DAIRY
☐ Buttermilk
☐ Sour cream: 1 (4-ounce) container

### SEAFOOD
☐ Crabmeat, 6 ounces

### CANNED
☐ Chickpeas: 1 (14-ounce) can

### GRAINS
☐ Quinoa: 2½ cups cooked (1 cup dry)

## YOUR LUNCHES THIS WEEK

| DAY | LUNCH |
|---|---|
| MONDAY | Crab and Mango–Stuffed Avocado |
| TUESDAY | Crab and Mango–Stuffed Avocado |
| WEDNESDAY | Quinoa and Veggie Bowl |
| THURSDAY | Quinoa and Veggie Bowl |
| FRIDAY | Quinoa and Veggie Bowl |

# STEP-BY-STEP PREP

1. In a pot, bring 1 cup of dry quinoa, 2 cups of water, and ½ teaspoon of sea salt to a boil. Reduce heat to low and cover. Simmer for 10 minutes. Fluff with a fork. Cool. (If using precooked quinoa, skip this step.)

2. Preheat your oven to 425°F. Roast the vegetables and chickpeas for the Quinoa and Veggie Bowls as instructed (page 44).

3. While vegetables cook, mix Ranch Dressing (page 145) for the Quinoa and Veggie Bowls. Separate into three small containers for lunches.

4. Halve the avocados lengthwise. Cut the lime in half. Set aside.

5. Rinse the crabmeat to remove any remaining bits of shell. Prepare the mixture for the Crab and Mango–Stuffed Avocado as instructed (page 45).

6. Assemble the Quinoa and Veggie Bowls (page 44).

7. Seal and refrigerate all meals.

# QUINOA AND VEGGIE BOWLS

GLUTEN-FREE, NUT-FREE, VEGETARIAN

*Servings: 3 / Prep time: 10 minutes / Cook time: 30 minutes*

Creamy Ranch Dressing adds a ton of flavor to this simple but nutritious quinoa-based lunch. Roasting the vegetables brings out deeply caramelized flavors in the vegetables that make this a complex and satisfying dish.

1¾ red onions, cut into ½-inch pieces

1 sweet potato, cut into ½-inch cubes (peeling optional)

1 red bell pepper, stem, seeds, and ribs removed, cut into ½-inch pieces

2 cups Brussels sprouts, halved

1 (15-ounce) can chickpeas, drained

2 tablespoons olive oil

½ teaspoon sea salt

⅛ teaspoon freshly cracked black pepper

1½ cups cooked quinoa, cooled

Ranch Dressing (page 145)

1. Preheat your oven to 425°F.

2. In a bowl, combine the red onions, sweet potato, bell pepper, Brussels sprouts, and chickpeas.

3. Add the olive oil, salt, and pepper for dressing. Toss to mix.

4. Spread in a single layer on two rimmed baking sheets. Bake in the preheated oven until the vegetables begin to brown, about 30 minutes. Stir once during cooking.

5. Cool the vegetables completely.

6. Evenly divide cooked quinoa and vegetables between three containers.

7. Store the dressing in three small containers. Toss the other ingredients with the dressing just before serving.

> **DIETARY SWAP:** To make this nonvegetarian, add 5 ounces of cooked salmon (or canned salmon) to each of the bowls.

Per Serving: Calories: 508; Total Fat: 22g; Saturated Fat: 4g; Cholesterol: 11mg; Carbohydrates: 65g; Fiber: 14g; Protein: 15g

# CRAB AND MANGO-STUFFED AVOCADO

DAIRY-FREE, GLUTEN-FREE, NUT-FREE

*Servings: 2 / Prep time: 10 minutes*

Cooked crab will keep in the fridge for about five days, so it's a good meat for lunch prep. You can also use imitation crab (krab), which is less expensive. Keep in mind though that krab contains gluten, so if you're going for gluten-free, you're better off substituting cooked baby shrimp or even shredded chicken breast for the crab. For best results, make the crab salad ahead of time and cut the avocado just before serving.

6 ounces cooked crabmeat, rinsed and picked over for shells

1 cup cooked quinoa, cooled

1 mango, peeled, pitted, and cut into cubes

¼ red onion, finely minced

½ teaspoon ground cumin

¼ teaspoon ground coriander

1 garlic clove, minced

½ teaspoon sea salt

Juice of 1 lime, divided

2 avocados

1. In a bowl, mix together the crabmeat, quinoa, mango, red onion, cumin, coriander, garlic, and salt. Add half of the lime juice. Stir to mix.

2. Slice the avocados in half lengthwise and remove the pits. Divide the halves evenly between two containers, with the avocados facing cut-side up. Pour the remaining lime juice over the cut part of the avocados.

3. Spoon the crab-and-mango mixture evenly into each of the avocado halves. Seal tightly.

> **DIETARY SWAP:** Make this vegetarian by replacing the crab with 6 ounces of canned hearts of palm.

Per Serving: Calories: 397; Total Fat: 14g; Saturated Fat: 2g; Cholesterol: 91mg; Carbohydrates: 54g; Fiber: 10g; Protein: 21g

Elote and Shrimp Salad
*Page 51*

# Chapter 7
# WEEK 5

Corn and shrimp take top billing this week and your simply delicious lunch prep meals include a soup and a salad. Roasting corn on the cob on a grill (if you've got one) and cutting the kernels with a sharp knife is the way to go for these recipes because the method imparts smoky, complex flavors that will be missing in your finished product without it. If you don't have a grill, you can also substitute canned or frozen corn, but adding about ½ teaspoon of smoked paprika to each recipe helps bring in the smoky flavors.

## SHOPPING LIST

The shopping list below is for the two recipes as written. Substitutions for making both recipes either vegetarian or meat-based are as follows:

* If adding meat to Corn Chowder, get 6 slices bacon.
* If making Elote and Shrimp Salad vegetarian, skip shrimp and increase quantity of corn to 11 ears (5½ cups, divided between the two recipes).

### PRODUCE
- Bell pepper, red: 1
- Cilantro, fresh: 1 bunch
- Corn, on the cob: 7 ears (or 3½ cups frozen or canned corn kernels)
- Fennel: 1 bulb
- Lime: 1
- Onion, red: 1
- Sweet potato: 1 medium

### DAIRY
- Cheese, cotija: ¼ cup (2 ounces) or grated Monterey Jack cheese

- Milk, almond or other plant-based
- Sour cream: 1 (4-ounce) container

### SEAFOOD
- Shrimp, baby (cooked): 8 ounces

### SPICES
- Smoked paprika or paprika

## YOUR LUNCHES THIS WEEK

| DAY | LUNCH |
|-----------|-----------------------------|
| MONDAY | **Elote and Shrimp Salad** |
| TUESDAY | **Elote and Shrimp Salad** |
| WEDNESDAY | **Sweet and Smoky Corn Chowder** |
| THURSDAY | **Sweet and Smoky Corn Chowder** |
| FRIDAY | **Sweet and Smoky Corn Chowder** |

# STEP-BY-STEP PREP

1. If using ears of corn, remove the husks and clean the corn. Rinse away any silk and pat the corn dry. Brush the corn with 1 tablespoon of melted butter or olive oil per cob. Season it liberally with salt, pepper, and 1 teaspoon of smoked paprika.

2. Preheat the grill to high for about 10 minutes. Then grill the corn, turning it several times, for 15 minutes until it is cooked and has some char showing in some areas. If using the oven instead, preheat it to 400°F and roast for 35–40 minutes. Cool.

3. Use a sharp knife to cut the kernels from the cob, and divide them for each recipe (1½ cups for chowder and 2 cups for elote).

4. Chop the vegetables and fresh herbs and set aside.

5. Cook the Sweet and Smoky Corn Chowder (page 50). Divide between three containers. Refrigerate.

6. Assemble the Elote and Shrimp Salad and toss with the dressing. Store as instructed.

# SWEET AND SMOKY CORN CHOWDER

DAIRY-FREE, NUT-FREE, VEGAN

*Servings: 3 / Prep time: 10 minutes / Cook time: 30 minutes*

The earthy sweetness of the sweet potatoes and corn brings an extra layer of depth to this creamy, delicious vegetarian chowder. It's best served warm, so heat it up in the morning and pack it in your thermos for a delicious, comforting lunch.

3 tablespoons olive oil

½ red onion, finely chopped

½ red bell pepper, stem, ribs, and seeds removed, chopped

1 fennel bulb, chopped

2 tablespoons all-purpose flour

4 cups vegetable broth

½ teaspoon garlic powder

1 teaspoon smoked paprika

1 teaspoon dried thyme

1 sweet potato, peeled and cut into cubes

½ teaspoon sea salt

⅛ teaspoon freshly cracked black pepper

1½ cups cooked corn (from about 3 ears of corn)

½ cup unsweetened nondairy milk, such as almond milk

½ bunch chopped fresh cilantro

1. In a large pot, heat the olive oil on medium-high heat until it shimmers.

2. Add the onion, red bell pepper, and fennel and cook, stirring frequently, until the vegetables are soft and begin to brown, 5 to 7 minutes.

3. Add the flour and cook, stirring constantly, for 1 minute.

4. Add the broth and use the side of a spoon to scrape any browned bits from the bottom of the pan.

5. Add the garlic powder, smoked paprika, thyme, sweet potato, salt, and pepper. Bring to a boil, stirring occasionally, and then reduce the heat to medium. Cook, stirring occasionally, until the potatoes are tender, about 5 minutes.

6. Stir in the corn and the milk. Cook, stirring, for 1 minute more to heat through.

7. Remove from heat and stir in the cilantro.

**DIETARY SWAP:** If you'd prefer to make a nonvegetarian option, instead of heating olive oil, cook 6 slices of bacon, cut into pieces, in the pot in step 1. When the bacon is browned and crisp, remove it from the pot with a slotted spoon and set it aside on a platter. Use the fat from the bacon to cook the vegetables and proceed with the recipe as written. Return the cooked bacon to the pot in step 6 or use it as a garnish.

Per Serving: Calories: 302; Total Fat: 15g; Saturated Fat: 2g; Cholesterol: 0mg; Carbohydrates: 39g; Fiber: 7.5g; Protein: 5g

# ELOTE AND SHRIMP SALAD

GLUTEN-FREE, NUT-FREE

*Servings: 2 / Prep time: 10 minutes*

Elote, or Mexican street corn, is a delicious, sweet, and smoky grilled corn dish. This salad invokes the flavors of elote and adds sweet cooked baby shrimp to provide protein. If you can't find cotija cheese (which will be in either the cheese or the Mexican section of the grocery store), you can use grated Parmesan, crumbled queso fresco, or crumbled feta cheese.

Cooked kernels from
　4 ears of corn or 2 cups of
　cooked corn

½ red onion, finely chopped

½ red bell pepper, stem,
　ribs, and seeds removed,
　finely minced

8 ounces cooked baby shrimp

½ bunch chopped
　fresh cilantro

½ cup sour cream or crema

Juice of 1 lime

½ teaspoon smoked paprika

¼ cup grated cotija cheese
　(or Monterey Jack cheese)

½ teaspoon sea salt

1. In a large bowl, combine the corn, red onion, bell pepper, shrimp, and cilantro. Toss.

2. In a small bowl, whisk together the sour cream, lime juice, smoked paprika, cotija cheese, and salt.

3. Toss the dressing with the salad and portion evenly into two containers. Refrigerate.

> **DIETARY SWAP:** Make this vegetarian by replacing the shrimp with an additional 2 cups of cooked corn.

Per Serving: Calories: 562; Total Fat: 30g; Saturated Fat: 11g; Cholesterol: 219mg; Carbohydrates: 50g; Fiber: 5g; Protein: 27g

51

Turkey Cauliflower Fried Rice
Page 57

# Chapter 8
# WEEK 6

Cauliflower and bell peppers are on deck for this week. Bell peppers add bright colors, a nice crunchy texture, and a slightly sweet peppery bite to your meals. When you prepare bell peppers, use a sharp knife to trim out the ribs and seeds from the center of the pepper. Feel free to substitute any colored bell pepper in both recipes.

Cauliflower is also a highly versatile ingredient, and it's become a popular, lower-carb substitute for rice, which is how it is used here. You can actually save time by purchasing precut cauliflower rice in the produce or frozen aisle of your local grocer. But it's super easy to make by either pulsing cauliflower florets in a food processor until they take on a rice-like texture or grating them on a box grater.

## SHOPPING LIST

The shopping list below is for the two recipes as written. Substitutions for making both recipes either vegetarian or meat-based are as follows:

* If adding meat to Tex-Mex Cauliflower-Stuffed Peppers, increase quantity of turkey to 20 ounces.
* If making Turkey Cauliflower Fried Rice vegetarian, skip turkey and double the amount of peas and eggs.

### PRODUCE
☐ Bell pepper, red or green: 3
☐ Carrot: 1
☐ Cauliflower: 1 head (or about 4 cups store-bought riced cauliflower)
☐ Cilantro: 1 bunch
☐ Peas, fresh or frozen: 1 cup
☐ Scallions: 1 bunch

### DAIRY & EGGS
☐ Pepper Jack cheese: 2 ounces
☐ Eggs: 2

### MEAT/POULTRY/FISH/PROTEIN
☐ Ground turkey: 12 ounces

### CANNED
☐ Beans, black: 1 (15-ounce) can
☐ Tomatoes, chopped: 1 (15-ounce) can

# YOUR LUNCHES THIS WEEK

| DAY | LUNCH |
| --- | --- |
| MONDAY | **Turkey Cauliflower Fried Rice** |
| TUESDAY | **Tex-Mex Cauliflower-Stuffed Peppers** |
| WEDNESDAY | **Turkey Cauliflower Fried Rice** |
| THURSDAY | **Tex-Mex Cauliflower-Stuffed Peppers** |
| FRIDAY | **Turkey Cauliflower Fried Rice** |

# STEP-BY-STEP PREP

1. Rice the cauliflower by grating on a box grater or pulsing the florets in a food processor (skip this step if using store-bought riced cauliflower). Set aside.

2. Chop the scallions. Peel and chop the carrot. Set aside.

3. Cut tops off of two peppers and remove the seeds and ribs. Set aside.

4. Remove seeds, stem, and ribs from the remaining red bell pepper. Chop along with the tops of the other two bell peppers, and separate about ¼ cup of the chopped bell pepper for the stuffed peppers and save the rest for the rice.

5. Grate the cheese. Set aside.

6. Cook the ground turkey in a skillet for about 5 minutes, crumbling with a spoon, until browned.

7. Prepare the Tex-Mex Cauliflower-Stuffed Peppers (page 56). Divide evenly between two containers. Refrigerate.

8. While the bell peppers bake, prepare the Turkey Cauliflower Fried Rice (page 57). Divide evenly between three containers. Refrigerate.

# TEX-MEX CAULIFLOWER-STUFFED PEPPERS

GLUTEN-FREE, NUT-FREE, VEGETARIAN

*Servings: 2 / Prep time: 20 minutes / Cook time: 1 hour*

Stuffed bell peppers are bright, colorful, and flavorful. This recipe uses Tex-Mex flavors that are really satisfying. You can add optional garnishes such as sour cream or guacamole to add even more flavor. Eat cold or reheat in the microwave or a regular oven.

2 tablespoons olive oil

2 red or green bell peppers, seeded and stems and ribs removed

½ bunch scallions, chopped

½ head cauliflower, grated or chopped into rice (about 2 cups)

1 (10-ounce) can chopped tomatoes and chiles (such as RO*TEL)

1 (15-ounce) can of black beans, drained

½ teaspoon chili powder

½ teaspoon ground cumin

½ teaspoon garlic powder

½ teaspoon ground coriander

½ teaspoon sea salt

½ cup grated Pepper Jack cheese

½ bunch chopped fresh cilantro

1. Preheat your oven to 350°F.

2. In a large skillet over medium-high heat, heat the olive oil until it shimmers. Add the chopped bell pepper and the scallions. Cook, stirring occasionally, until the vegetables soften, about 5 minutes.

3. Add the cauliflower and cook, stirring, for 3 minutes more.

4. Add the tomatoes, black beans, chili powder, cumin, garlic powder, coriander, and salt. Bring to a simmer. Reduce the heat to medium-low and cook, stirring occasionally, until the tomatoes thicken, about 5 minutes.

5. Put the hollowed-out bell peppers onto a rimmed baking sheet cut-side up. Spoon the cauliflower mixture evenly into the peppers and sprinkle with the cheese.

6. Cover with foil and bake in the oven for 40 minutes. Remove the foil and continue to bake for 20 minutes more, until the cheese is browned and bubbly. Sprinkle with the cilantro.

> **DIETARY SWAP:** To make this nonvegetarian, brown 8 ounces of ground turkey and mix it into the cauliflower rice in place of the black beans.

Per Serving: Calories: 549; Total Fat: 23g; Saturated Fat: 7.5g; Cholesterol: 25mg; Carbohydrates: 63g; Fiber: 23g; Protein: 26g

# TURKEY CAULIFLOWER FRIED RICE

DAIRY-FREE, NUT-FREE

*Servings: 3 / Prep time: 10 minutes / Cook time: 15 minutes*

Cauliflower fried rice is low in carbs and delicious. This recipe also makes a delicious side dish for dinners, and it will freeze well, so feel free to make a large batch and store it in single servings in the freezer. You can also substitute ground beef, ground chicken, or ground pork in place of the turkey.

12 ounces ground turkey

2 tablespoons olive oil

½ bunch scallions, chopped

1 red or green bell pepper, stem, seeds, and ribs removed, chopped

1 carrot, chopped

2 eggs, beaten

½ head cauliflower, riced (about 2 cups)

1 cup fresh or frozen peas

3 tablespoons reduced-sodium soy sauce

½ teaspoon ground ginger

½ teaspoon garlic powder

½ bunch chopped fresh cilantro

1. In a large skillet or wok, cook the ground turkey over medium-high heat, crumbling with a spoon until browned, 5 to 7 minutes. Remove the turkey from the skillet and set it aside. Wipe out the skillet with a paper towel and return it to the heat.

2. Heat the olive oil over medium-high heat until it shimmers.

3. Add the scallions, red bell pepper, and carrot. Cook, stirring occasionally, until the vegetables are soft, about 5 minutes.

4. Add the egg and cook, stirring, until the eggs set, about two minutes more.

5. Add the cauliflower rice and the peas.

6. In a small bowl, whisk together the soy sauce, ginger, and garlic powder. Add to the rice. Cook, stirring, for 5 minutes more.

7. Remove from heat and stir in cilantro. Divide evenly between three containers and refrigerate.

> **DIETARY SWAP:** To make this vegetarian, omit the turkey and skip step 1. Instead, add one more cup (2 cups total) of peas and 2 more eggs (4 total) beaten.

Per Serving: Calories: 400; Total Fat: 21g; Saturated Fat: 4.5g; Cholesterol: 200mg; Carbohydrates: 20g; Fiber: 7g; Protein: 34g

Greek-Inspired Pasta Salad

*Page 62*

*Chapter 9*
# WEEK 7

Feta cheese and olives are stepping up this week, adding a savory element to dishes while also incorporating healthy fats. You can use simple canned olives or get fancy and hit up the olive bar at the grocery store. Feta is a crumbled sheep or goat cheese with a distinctly sharp and salty flavor that's delicious in both of these meal prep recipes.

## SHOPPING LIST

The shopping list below is for the two recipes as written. Substitutions for making both recipes either vegetarian or meat-based are as follows:

* If adding meat to Greek-Inspired Pasta Salad, get 1 (5-ounce) can of tuna.
* If making Bacon, Feta, and Olive Crustless Quiche Cups vegetarian, skip bacon and get 1 red bell pepper.

### PRODUCE
☐ Garlic: 1 bulb
☐ Lemon: 1
☐ Onion, red: 1
☐ Parsley, Italian: 1 bunch

### DAIRY & EGGS
☐ Cheese, feta: 4 ounces
☐ Eggs: 8 (should have left over from last week)
☐ Milk: 1 small container

### MEAT
☐ Bacon, thick sliced: 6 slices (or 10 thin-sliced pieces)

### CANNED/BOXED
☐ Artichoke hearts, unmarinated: 1 (10-ounce) jar
☐ Bell pepper, red, roasted: 1 (10-ounce) jar
☐ Olives, black, sliced: 2 (2.25-ounce) cans
☐ Pasta, rotini (or another pasta of your choice): 1 8-ounce box

## YOUR LUNCHES THIS WEEK

| DAY | LUNCH |
|---|---|
| MONDAY | **Bacon, Feta, and Olive Crustless Quiche Cups** |
| TUESDAY | **Greek-Inspired Pasta Salad** |
| WEDNESDAY | **Bacon, Feta, and Olive Crustless Quiche Cups** |
| THURSDAY | **Greek-Inspired Pasta Salad** |
| FRIDAY | **Bacon, Feta, and Olive Crustless Quiche Cups** |

# STEP-BY-STEP PREP

1. Cook, drain, and cool the pasta. Freeze any pasta you won't be using this week in 1-cup servings.

2. Open and drain olives, artichoke hearts, and roasted red bell peppers.

3. Chop the red onion and parsley and set aside.

4. Zest and juice the lemon.

5. Prepare Bacon, Feta, and Olive Crustless Quiche Cups (page 63).

6. While quiches bake, prepare the Greek-Inspired Pasta Salad (page 62).

# GREEK-INSPIRED PASTA SALAD

NUT-FREE, VEGETARIAN

*Servings: 2 / Prep time: 20 minutes*

Pasta is a great meal prep item. You can make a whole box of pasta ahead of time and then freeze the cooked pasta in 1-cup servings to thaw for use during meal prep. For rotini pasta, about ½ cup of dry pasta yields one cup of cooked pasta. If you use olives from the olive bar instead of canned olives, don't forget to remove the pits and discard them.

2 cups of cooked rotini pasta (from 1 cup dry), drained and cooled

1 (2.25-ounce) can sliced black olives, drained

1 (12-ounce) jar unmarinated artichoke hearts, quartered

1 (12-ounce) jar roasted red bell peppers, drained and chopped

½ red onion, minced

½ bunch fresh Italian parsley, chopped

½ cup (2 ounces) feta cheese

¼ cup extra-virgin olive oil

Grated zest and juice of 1 lemon

1 teaspoon Dijon mustard

2 garlic cloves, minced

½ teaspoon sea salt

Pinch red pepper flakes

⅛ teaspoon freshly cracked black pepper

1. In a large bowl, combine the pasta, olives, artichoke hearts, roasted red bell peppers, red onion, parsley, and feta. Mix well.

2. In a small bowl, whisk together the olive oil, lemon zest and juice, Dijon mustard, garlic, salt, red pepper flakes, and pepper.

3. Toss with the pasta salad.

4. Divide the pasta salad evenly between two containers. Refrigerate.

> **SUBSTITUTION TIP:** To make this nonvegetarian, add 1 (5-ounce) can of water-packed tuna, drained. Add it in step 1.

Per Serving: Calories: 798; Total Fat: 39g; Saturated Fat: 8g; Cholesterol: 20mg; Carbohydrates: 77g; Fiber: 13g; Protein: 24g

# BACON, FETA, AND OLIVE CRUSTLESS QUICHE CUPS

GLUTEN-FREE, NUT-FREE

*Servings: 3 (2 quiche cups per serving) / Prep time: 10 minutes / Cook time: 35 minutes*

Use a six-cup muffin tin to create these crustless quiche cups. They freeze quite well, so feel free to double the batch and freeze them in a zipper bag for up to two months.

Nonstick cooking spray (optional)

6 slices thick-cut bacon

½ red onion, minced

3 garlic cloves, minced

8 eggs, beaten

¼ cup milk

½ teaspoon sea salt

⅛ teaspoon freshly cracked black pepper

1 teaspoon dried thyme

1 (2.25-ounce) can sliced black olives, drained

½ cup (2 ounces) crumbled feta cheese

½ bunch chopped fresh Italian parsley

1. Preheat oven to 350°F. Spray a six-cup muffin tin with nonstick cooking spray or line the muffin with silicone muffin liners.

2. In a skillet, cook the bacon until browned and crisp, about 6 minutes. Remove the bacon from the fat in the pan, blot it with a paper towel, crumble it, and set it aside.

3. Remove all but 2 tablespoons of bacon fat from the skillet. Add the red onion and cook, stirring occasionally, until the onion is soft, about 5 minutes. Add the garlic and cook, stirring constantly, for 30 seconds. Cool.

4. In a large bowl, whisk together the eggs, milk, salt, pepper, and thyme until well blended.

5. Fold in the reserved bacon and add the onions, garlic, olives, feta, and parsley.

6. Pour into the prepared muffin tins. Bake in the preheated oven until puffy and solid, about 35 minutes.

> **COOKING TIP:** To make this vegetarian, omit the bacon and skip step 2. Instead, add 1 chopped red bell pepper and 2 tablespoons of olive oil. Heat the olive oil in place of the bacon fat in step 3 on medium-high heat until it shimmers, and then cook the red bell pepper and onion. Continue with the recipe as written.

Per Serving: Calories: 450; Total Fat: 32g; Saturated Fat: 11g; Cholesterol: 533mg; Carbohydrates: 8g; Fiber: 1g; Protein: 27g

Rotisserie Chicken and
Shaved Fennel Salad
*Page 69*

# Chapter 10
# WEEK 8

65

Lemon and fennel play the central role in this week's recipes. Lemon adds bright flavors and acidity to foods along with a nice dose of vitamin C. The juice adds a hint of lemon, while the zest adds a more bold flavor. To zest a lemon, use a rasp-style grater and grate just the yellow part of the lemon peel, leaving the bitter white part, called the pith, on the lemon. Juice lemons through a strainer to easily remove seeds.

Fennel looks a lot like celery with feathery fronds. You can eat either the fennel bulb or cut the fronds up to sprinkle on finished dishes to give them a fresh herb flavor. You'll find fennel in the produce section of your grocery store labeled either as fennel or anise. It's delicious raw or cooked.

## SHOPPING LIST

The shopping list below is for the two recipes as written. Substitutions for making both recipes either vegetarian or meat-based are as follows:

* If adding meat to Fennel Avgolemono Soup, use leftover rotisserie chicken.
* If making Fennel Salad vegetarian, skip chicken and get 3 cups tempeh.

### PRODUCE
☐ Apples, sweet-tart: 2
☐ Fennel, whole: 3
☐ Garlic, bulb: 1
☐ Lemon: 3
☐ Onion, red: 1
☐ Shallot: 1

### DAIRY & EGGS
☐ Eggs: 2

### POULTRY
☐ Chicken, cooked, rotisserie: 1

## YOUR LUNCHES THIS WEEK

| DAY | LUNCH |
|---|---|
| MONDAY | **Rotisserie Chicken and Shaved Fennel Salad** |
| TUESDAY | **Fennel Avgolemono Soup** |
| WEDNESDAY | **Rotisserie Chicken and Shaved Fennel Salad** |
| THURSDAY | **Fennel Avgolemono Soup** |
| FRIDAY | **Rotisserie Chicken and Shaved Fennel Salad** |

# STEP-BY-STEP PREP

1. If roasting a chicken, roast it in a roasting pan in a 350°F oven until it reaches an internal temperature of 165°F, about 90 minutes. Cool completely.

2. Remove skin from chicken. Remove the chicken from the bones and chop it. Measure out three cups and freeze any left over for use in another recipe.

3. Cut stalks from fennel bulbs and cut the fronds from the stalks. Chop the fronds and discard or freeze the stalks for another use.

4. Remove the cores from the fennel bulbs and discard them. Shave 2 fennel bulbs on a mandoline or the slicing attachment of a food processor. Chop the third fennel bulb.

5. Peel and julienne the apples, peel and slice the red onion, and mince the garlic and shallot. Set aside.

6. Zest and juice the lemons, measuring the correct amount of juice and zest for each recipe. Whisk egg yolks together with juice of 2 lemons.

7. Whisk together the Lemon-Dijon Vinaigrette (page 152)

8. Prepare Fennel Avgolemono Soup (page 68).

9. While the soup cooks, prepare Rotisserie Chicken and Shaved Fennel Salad (page 69).

67

# FENNEL AVGOLEMONO SOUP

DAIRY-FREE, GLUTEN-FREE, NUT-FREE, VEGETARIAN

*Servings: 2 / Prep time: 10 minutes / Cook time: 20 minutes*

Avgolemono is a Greek soup that finishes with bright lemon flavors from a lemon juice and egg mixture you stir in after heating the soup. The egg yolks will thicken the soup while the lemon juice adds a fresh, bright character.

2 tablespoons olive oil

½ red onion, finely chopped

1 fennel bulb, core removed, and chopped

6 garlic cloves, minced

4 cups low-sodium vegetable broth

½ teaspoon sea salt

¼ teaspoon freshly cracked black pepper

Juice of 2 freshly squeezed lemons

2 egg yolks

1 tablespoon chopped fresh fennel fronds

1 teaspoon grated lemon zest

1. In a large pot, heat the olive oil over medium-high heat until it shimmers.

2. Add the red onion and fennel and cook, stirring occasionally, until the vegetables begin to soften and slightly brown, 5 to 7 minutes.

3. Add the garlic and cook, stirring constantly, for 30 seconds.

4. Add the vegetable broth, salt, and pepper. Bring to a simmer and reduce the heat to medium-low. Simmer, stirring occasionally, for 5 minutes.

5. In a small bowl, whisk together the lemon juice and the egg yolks.

6. Pour into the soup in a thin stream, stirring. Simmer, stirring, for about 5 minutes, until the soup thickens.

7. Remove from the heat and stir in the chopped fennel fronds and the lemon zest. Let cool.

8. Divide the soup evenly between two containers and refrigerate.

> **SUBSTITUTION TIP:** To make this nonvegetarian, add 1 cup of shredded chicken from the rotisserie chicken (with the bones and skin removed) in step 4.

Per Serving: Calories: 249; Total Fat: 18g; Saturated Fat: 3.5g; Cholesterol: 184mg; Carbohydrates: 17g; Fiber: 3g; Protein: 6g

# ROTISSERIE CHICKEN AND SHAVED FENNEL SALAD

DAIRY-FREE, GLUTEN-FREE, NUT-FREE

*Servings: 3 / Prep time: 10 minutes*

Purchasing a grocery store rotisserie chicken is the quickest way for this simple salad to come together. Simply remove the meat from the skin and bones and chop it. Then, store any leftover chicken in 1-cup serving sizes (a whole chicken has about 3 cups total of boneless, skinless meat) in the freezer for use in salads or other recipes. You can shave the fennel bulb on a mandoline or the shaving blades of a box grater or food processor.

2 fennel bulbs, cores removed and shaved

2 sweet-tart apples (such as Granny Smith or Braeburn), peeled and julienned

2 tablespoons chopped fennel fronds

½ red onion, very thinly sliced

3 cups chopped boneless and skinless rotisserie chicken

Lemon-Dijon Vinaigrette (page 152)

1. In a large bowl, combine the fennel bulbs, apples, fennel fronds, red onion, and chicken. Toss to mix.

2. Divide salad evenly between three containers and refrigerate. Toss with ⅓ of a recipe of the Lemon-Dijon Vinaigrette just before eating.

> **COOKING TIP:** To make this vegetarian, omit the chicken. Instead, replace it with 3 cups of chopped tempeh.

Per Serving: Calories: 418; Total Fat: 17g; Saturated Fat: 4g; Cholesterol: 120mg; Carbohydrates: 31g; Fiber: 8.5g; Protein: 39g

Tofu and Veggie Lettuce
Wraps with Walnut Sauce
*Page 74*

# Chapter 11
# WEEK 9

**TOFU AND VEGGIE LETTUCE WRAPS WITH WALNUT SAUCE** 74

**WALNUT-CRUSTED SALMON WITH CITRUS-YOGURT SAUCE** 76

Smooth, creamy, protein-filled Greek yogurt and crunchy, flavorful walnuts are the standout ingredients this week. The walnuts are a great source of omega-3 fatty acids while Greek yogurt is a particularly substantial, high-protein type of yogurt, so both are nutritional powerhouses. This week's lunches are a study in textural contrasts, as well, so they're super satisfying for people who like creamy and crunchy textures side by side in their meals.

## SHOPPING LIST

The shopping list below is for the two recipes as written. Substitutions for making both recipes either vegetarian or meat-based are as follows:

* If adding meat to Tofu and Veggie Lettuce Wraps, increase quantity of salmon to 16 ounces.
* If making Walnut-Crusted Salmon vegetarian, skip salmon and get 1 eggplant.

### PRODUCE
- ☐ Bean sprouts: 1 cup
- ☐ Bell pepper, red: 1
- ☐ Carrots: 3
- ☐ Cilantro: 1 bunch
- ☐ Dill: 1 bunch
- ☐ Garlic: 1 bulb
- ☐ Ginger root: small piece
- ☐ Lemon: 1
- ☐ Lettuce, butter: 1 head
- ☐ Limes: 3
- ☐ Mushrooms, shiitake: 8 ounces
- ☐ Orange: 1
- ☐ Scallions: 1 bunch

### DAIRY & EGGS
- ☐ Yogurt, Greek, plain: 12 ounces

### FISH/PROTEIN
- ☐ Salmon: 8 ounces
- ☐ Tofu, extra-firm: 8 ounces

### OTHER
- ☐ Bread crumbs: ¼ cup
- ☐ Sesame oil: 1 bottle
- ☐ Walnuts: ¾ cup

## YOUR LUNCHES THIS WEEK

| DAY | LUNCH |
|---|---|
| MONDAY | **Tofu and Veggie Lettuce Wraps with Walnut Sauce** |
| TUESDAY | **Walnut-Crusted Salmon with Citrus-Yogurt Sauce** |
| WEDNESDAY | **Tofu and Veggie Lettuce Wraps with Walnut Sauce** |
| THURSDAY | **Walnut-Crusted Salmon with Citrus-Yogurt Sauce** |
| FRIDAY | **Tofu and Veggie Lettuce Wraps with Walnut Sauce** |

# STEP-BY-STEP PREP

1. Zest and juice the citrus fruits and set aside.

2. Mix the marinade and marinate tofu for 30 minutes.

3. Use tweezers to remove the pin bones from the salmon.

4. Crust salmon (see Walnut-Crusted Salmon with Citrus-Yogurt Sauce on page 76) and roast.

5. While salmon roasts, chop the vegetables and set aside.

6. Cook the tofu with mushrooms (see Tofu and Veggie Lettuce Wraps with Walnut Sauce on page 74). Cool.

7. Cool the salmon.

8. Mix vegetables for lettuce wraps (page 74), sauce for lettuce wraps (page 74), and sauce for salmon (page 76).

# TOFU AND VEGGIE LETTUCE WRAPS WITH WALNUT SAUCE

VEGETARIAN

*Servings: 3 / Prep time: 10 minutes / Cook time: 10 minutes*

Lettuce wraps make a great meal prep lunch. Butter lettuce has large leaves, and it also is flexible and tender, so it's the perfect lettuce to make wraps. You could also replace the butter lettuce leaves with napa cabbage leaves, which will have a bit more crunch, or large kale leaves, depending on what's locally available and in season.

2 tablespoons reduced-sodium soy sauce

Juice of 3 limes, divided (about 6 tablespoons)

1 teaspoon grated ginger root

2 garlic cloves, minced, divided

2 teaspoons sriracha (or your preferred hot sauce), divided

8 ounces extra-firm tofu, cut into ½-inch pieces

2 tablespoons olive oil

8 ounces shiitake mushrooms, stems removed, sliced

3 carrots, julienned

1 bunch scallions, sliced

1 cup bean sprouts

1 red bell pepper, stem, rib, and seeds removed, julienned

1. In a small bowl, whisk together the soy sauce, juice of 2 limes, ginger root, 1 minced garlic clove, and 1 teaspoon of sriracha. Add the tofu and mix to coat. Allow tofu to marinate for at least 30 minutes.

2. Remove the tofu from the marinade and pat it dry with a paper towel.

3. In a wok or large skillet, heat the olive oil over medium-high heat until it shimmers.

4. Add the tofu and mushrooms and cook, stirring occasionally, until the mushrooms are browned, 5 to 7 minutes. Cool and set aside.

5. In a bowl, combine the carrots, scallions, bean sprouts, red bell pepper, and cilantro. Toss to mix. Set aside.

6. In a medium bowl, whisk together the crushed walnuts, Greek yogurt, sesame oil, remaining juice of 1 lime, remaining minced garlic clove, and the remaining 1 teaspoon of sriracha. Portion into three small containers and refrigerate.

¼ cup chopped fresh cilantro

¼ cup walnuts, crushed

1 cup plain whole-milk
   Greek yogurt

¼ teaspoon sesame oil

9 large butter lettuce leaves

7. Fill three containers with the cooled tofu-and-mushroom mix, the mixed vegetables, and three lettuce leaves each. Refrigerate.

8. To assemble, spoon the veggies and tofu into lettuce leaves and use the walnut sauce as a dipping sauce.

> **DIETARY SWAP:** To make this nonvegetarian, replace the tofu with 8 ounces of canned or fresh salmon, skin removed.

Per Serving: Calories: 403; Total Fat: 24g; Saturated Fat: 4.5g; Cholesterol: 11mg; Carbohydrates: 30g; Fiber: 8.5g; Protein: 23g

# WALNUT-CRUSTED SALMON WITH CITRUS-YOGURT SAUCE

*Servings: 2 / Prep time: 10 minutes / Cook time: 20 minutes*

This savory salmon dish has a lovely crunch from the crust, and it blends beautifully with the creamy, bright citrus-and-herb yogurt sauce. You can serve the salmon chilled or heat it up in the microwave for a minute or two at lunchtime. You may wish to pack a simple side salad to round out your meal.

½ cup walnuts, finely chopped

¼ cup bread crumbs

1 teaspoon grated orange zest plus the juice of 1 orange, divided

1 teaspoon sea salt, divided

¼ teaspoon freshly cracked black pepper, divided

2 (4-ounce) salmon fillets, bones removed

2 teaspoons Dijon mustard

½ cup plain whole-milk Greek yogurt

Juice of 1 lemon

1 tablespoon chopped fresh dill

1. Preheat the oven to 350°F. Line a baking sheet with parchment paper.

2. In a small bowl, combine the walnuts, bread crumbs, orange zest, ½ teaspoon of the salt, and ⅛ teaspoon of the pepper. Mix well.

3. Place the salmon, skin-side down, on the prepared baking sheet.

4. Spread each piece with 1 teaspoon of the mustard.

5. Press half of the walnut mixture onto the top of each piece of fish.

6. Bake in the preheated oven until the salmon is opaque, about 20 minutes. Remove and let cool. Then, divide it evenly between two containers.

7. In a small bowl, whisk together the yogurt, lemon juice, orange juice, the remaining ½ teaspoon of salt and ⅛ teaspoon of pepper, and the dill. Divide between two containers.

8. To serve, spoon the sauce over the chilled or warmed salmon.

> **DIETARY SWAP:** Replace the salmon with 4 thick slices of eggplant. Increase cooking time to about 35 minutes, until the eggplant is soft.

Per Serving: Calories: 501; Total Fat: 29g; Saturated Fat: 4.5g; Cholesterol: 80mg; Carbohydrates: 24g; Fiber: 2.5g; Protein: 38g

Roasted Root
Vegetable Bowls
Page 82

# Chapter 12
## WEEK 10

79

Sweet potatoes are the perfect ingredient for so many reasons, including how deeply satisfying and filling they are, as well as their nutritional value. Your other star ingredient this week is shallots, a type of onion used to bring bold flavors to many dishes including barbecue sauces and salad dressings. When roasted as they are in the Roasted Root Vegetable Bowls (page 82), they are mellow and sweet, or they bring a flavorful tang to Pulled Pork–Stuffed Sweet Potatoes (page 83).

## SHOPPING LIST

The shopping list below is for the two recipes as written. Substitutions for making both recipes either vegetarian or meat-based are as follows:

* If adding meat to Roasted Root Vegetable Bowls, get 1 rotisserie chicken.
* If making Pulled Pork-Stuffed Sweet Potatoes vegetarian, skip ribs and get 12 ounces tempeh instead.

### PRODUCE

- ☐ Carrots: 4
- ☐ Fennel bulb: 1
- ☐ Shallots: 11
- ☐ Sweet potatoes, medium: 5

### OTHER

- ☐ Liquid smoke: 1 bottle
- ☐ Rice, brown, cooked: 1 cup (or ½ cup uncooked)
- ☐ Tomato sauce: 1 (14-ounce) can

### MEAT

- ☐ Pork, ribs, country style boneless: 1 pound

## YOUR LUNCHES THIS WEEK

| DAY | LUNCH |
| --- | --- |
| MONDAY | **Pulled Pork–Stuffed Sweet Potatoes** |
| TUESDAY | **Roasted Root Vegetable Bowls** |
| WEDNESDAY | **Pulled Pork–Stuffed Sweet Potatoes** |
| THURSDAY | **Roasted Root Vegetable Bowls** |
| FRIDAY | **Pulled Pork–Stuffed Sweet Potatoes** |

# STEP-BY-STEP PREP

1. Cook the pork in the slow cooker as described in Pulled Pork–Stuffed Sweet Potatoes (page 83).

2. Cook the rice according to package instructions (or thaw frozen cooked rice you already have).

3. Peel and chop the root vegetables.

4. Preheat the oven to 425°F. Prick the whole sweet potatoes with a fork and roast for about 50 minutes. Roast the chopped root vegetables for 20 minutes and cool.

5. While the vegetables roast, make the Sweet and Spicy Barbecue Sauce (page 147) and mix with the cooked pork. Cool.

6. Assemble the Roasted Root Vegetable Bowls (page 82).

7. Assemble the Pulled Pork–Stuffed Sweet Potatoes (page 83).

# ROASTED ROOT VEGETABLE BOWLS

DAIRY-FREE, GLUTEN-FREE, NUT-FREE, VEGAN

*Servings: 2 / Prep time: 10 minutes / Cook time: 40 minutes*

Roasted root vegetables are delicious warm or cool. They develop a deeply caramelized flavor with time in the oven that adds complexity to this simple and delicious dish. If you'd like, you can substitute an equal amount of cooked quinoa for the cooked brown rice. Whenever possible, make cooked grains like quinoa or brown rice ahead in large batches and freeze in 1-cup (two-serving) amounts in a sealed container.

2 sweet potatoes, cut into ¾-inch pieces

6 shallots, peeled and quartered lengthwise

4 carrots, cut into ¾-inch pieces

1 fennel bulb, cored and cut into ¾-inch pieces

2 tablespoons olive oil

½ teaspoon sea salt

⅛ teaspoon freshly cracked black pepper

1 teaspoon dried thyme

1 cup cooked brown rice

1. Preheat the oven to 425°F.

2. In a large bowl, combine the sweet potatoes, shallots, carrots, fennel, olive oil, salt, pepper, and thyme. Toss to mix.

3. Place in a single layer on two rimmed baking sheets.

4. Bake in the preheated oven for 20 minutes. Turn the vegetables and continue baking for another 20 minutes or until browned. Cool.

5. Divide the cooked rice evenly between two containers, and divide the vegetables evenly on top of the rice. Refrigerate.

> **DIETARY SWAP:** To make this nonvegetarian, add 4 ounces of cooked rotisserie chicken (boneless and skinless) to the bowls when you refrigerate them.

Per Serving: Calories: 534; Total Fat: 15g; Saturated Fat: 2g; Cholesterol: 0mg; Carbohydrates: 94g; Fiber: 17g; Protein: 11g

# PULLED PORK-STUFFED SWEET POTATOES

DAIRY-FREE, GLUTEN-FREE, NUT-FREE

*Servings: 3 / Prep time: 10 minutes / Cook time: 8 hours*

Make the pulled pork in a slow cooker for 8 to 12 hours on Saturday and refrigerate it overnight or make it during the day on Sunday and prep your meals in the evening. You can use a prepared barbecue sauce from the grocery store or our homemade Sweet and Spicy Barbecue Sauce. You can make a double or triple batch of the pork and freeze it for use in later recipes as well, since it freezes very well.

1 pound boneless country-style pork ribs

4 shallots, peeled and thinly sliced

½ teaspoon sea salt

⅛ teaspoon freshly cracked black pepper

¼ cup water or broth

½ cup Sweet and Spicy Barbecue Sauce (page 147)

3 sweet potatoes

1. In a slow cooker, combine the pork ribs, shallots, salt, pepper, and water. Cover and cook on low for 8 hours.

2. Shred the pork with a fork and mix with the barbecue sauce.

3. Meanwhile, preheat the oven to 425°F. Prick the sweet potatoes with a fork and roast in the preheated oven until soft, about 50 minutes. Cool.

4. Split the potatoes with a fork or a knife and place each potato in its own container. Spoon the pork into each potato and refrigerate.

> **DIETARY SWAP:** To make this vegetarian, omit steps 1 and 2. Instead, heat 2 tablespoons of olive oil in a pan and cook 12 ounces of tempeh cut into thin strips and the sliced shallots in the oil for 5 minutes, stirring. Add the barbecue sauce and cool. Then continue the recipe as directed.

Per Serving: Calories: 533; Total Fat: 13g; Saturated Fat: 4.5g; Cholesterol: 124mg; Carbohydrates: 54g; Fiber: 6g; Protein: 48g

# Part II

## BONUS MEAL PREP RECIPES

# Chapter 13
# LUNCHES

▶

# MUSTARD CHICKEN AND POTATO STIR-FRY

DAIRY-FREE, GLUTEN-FREE, NUT-FREE

*Servings: 4 / Prep time: 10 minutes / Cook time: 20 minutes*

While many people associate stir-fries with Asian flavor profiles, you can make a stir-fry with any flavors you like. If you have a wok, it's the ideal tool for making a stir-fry, but you can also use a large skillet or even a large pot if you need. Store in single servings in the fridge for up to five days or in the freezer for up to six months.

2 tablespoons olive oil

4 slices bacon, chopped

1 pound boneless, skinless chicken breast

1 onion, chopped

2 potatoes, peeled and cut into ½-inch pieces

1 bunch kale, chopped

¼ cup dry white wine or low-sodium chicken broth

1 tablespoon Dijon mustard

½ teaspoon garlic powder

½ teaspoon dried thyme

½ teaspoon sea salt

¼ teaspoon freshly cracked black pepper

1. In a large skillet or wok, heat the olive oil over medium-high heat until it shimmers.

2. Add the bacon and cook, stirring occasionally, until it is browned and crisp, about 4 minutes. Remove the bacon from the fat in the pan with a slotted spoon and set it aside on paper towels to drain.

3. Add the chicken to the oil in the pan and cook, stirring occasionally, until it is cooked through, 5 to 7 minutes. Remove it from the fat in the pan with the slotted spoon and set it aside.

4. Add the onion, potatoes, and kale. Cook, stirring occasionally, until the potatoes are fork-tender, about 7 minutes. Return chicken and bacon to the pan.

5. In a small bowl, whisk together the white wine or broth, mustard, garlic powder, dried thyme, salt, and pepper. Add the mixture to the pan and bring to a simmer. Cook, stirring, until the sauce thickens, about 3 minutes more. Remove from heat. Let cool.

6. Divide evenly between four containers. Refrigerate.

Per Serving: Calories: 436; Total Fat: 22g; Saturated Fat: 5.5g; Cholesterol: 101mg; Carbohydrates: 23g; Fiber: 5.5g; Protein: 34g

# GRILLED PESTO FLATBREAD WITH EGGS

*Servings: 5 / Prep time: 10 minutes / Cook time: 20 minutes*

If you don't want to make the flatbread yourself, you can save time by purchasing store-bought flatbreads or even premade pitas or tortillas. You can save additional time by purchasing store-bought pesto instead of making your own, although preparing pesto fresh always makes for better, fresher flavor. Store the uncooked flatbread dough in zipper bags in individual-serving portions in the freezer and thaw before cooking.

## For the flatbread

1½ cups flour

1 teaspoon baking powder

½ teaspoon sea salt

½ cup very cold water

1½ tablespoons olive oil, plus additional to grease the grill

## For the pesto

½ cup packed basil leaves

3 garlic cloves, minced

¼ cup freshly grated Parmesan cheese

¼ cup pine nuts

¼ cup olive oil

¼ teaspoon sea salt

Pinch red pepper flakes

## For the eggs

2 tablespoons olive oil

5 eggs

Salt and pepper for seasoning

## To make the flatbread

1. Heat a grill or grill pan over medium-high heat.

2. In a large bowl, mix the flour, baking powder, and salt. Stir in the cold water and oil to make a dough.

3. Divide into five pieces. Roll each into a ball and flatten into a ½-inch-thick circle.

4. Brush the grill with oil and cook the flatbread on it. Grill on both sides until browned, 3 to 4 minutes per side.

## To make the pesto

5. In a blender or food processor, combine all ingredients. Pulse 1-second pulses 10 to 20 times, until everything is finely chopped and mixed.

## To make the eggs

6. In a nonstick skillet, heat the olive oil over medium-low heat until it shimmers.

7. Crack the eggs into the pan. Season with the salt and pepper.

8. Cook until the whites are set, about 4 minutes.

9. Turn the heat off and flip the eggs. Allow to rest for 30 seconds for over easy or 1 minute for over medium.

10. To assemble, spread the pesto evenly onto each cooked flatbread and top with egg.

11. Once cool, store the flatbreads in five individual containers. Refrigerate.

> **COOKING TIP:** Keep your egg yolks from breaking. Crack the eggs on a flat surface, such as the counter, using a gentle tap, and hold the eggs very close to the surface as you crack them. Do not crack the eggs along an edge, such as on the rim of a pan.

Per Serving: Calories: 453; Total Fat: 31g; Saturated Fat: 5.5g; Cholesterol: 189mg; Carbohydrates: 31g; Fiber: 1.5g; Protein: 12g

# CHICKEN MEATBALLS

NUT-FREE

*Servings: 4 / Prep time: 10 minutes / Cook time: 20 minutes*

The trick to making moist and tender meatballs is using something called a panade, which is simply a combination of starch and dairy—in this case, bread crumbs and milk. You can even use a nondairy milk if you don't do dairy or a gluten-free bread crumb if you can't have gluten. For best results, make your bread crumbs from fresh bread instead of using commercially available bread crumbs. Tear the bread into pieces and place them in a blender or food processor and pulse until they make crumbs. Store in the freezer for up to six months or in the fridge for up to five days.

½ cup bread crumbs

½ cup milk

1 pound ground chicken

1 tablespoon Dijon mustard

1 teaspoon dried thyme

½ teaspoon Worcestershire sauce

1 teaspoon garlic powder

1 teaspoon onion powder

Dash of hot sauce

¼ teaspoon freshly cracked black pepper

1. Preheat the oven to 350°F. Line a rimmed baking sheet with parchment paper.

2. In a large bowl, combine the bread crumbs and milk, mixing well. Allow the mixture to sit for 5 minutes.

3. Add the chicken, mustard, thyme, Worcestershire sauce, garlic powder, onion powder, hot sauce, and pepper. Mix well.

4. Form into 1-inch balls and place them on the prepared baking sheet. Bake in the preheated oven until the meatballs reach an internal temperature of 165°F, about 20 minutes.

5. Let cool and divide evenly into four containers. Refrigerate.

> **SERVING SUGGESTION:** Make a meal out of this by serving with cooked brown rice (½ cup per serving) or by putting each meatball in half a pita with chopped kale and tomatoes.

Per Serving: Calories: 306; Total Fat: 13g; Saturated Fat: 3.5g; Cholesterol: 107mg; Carbohydrates: 12g; Fiber: 0.5g; Protein: 34g

# CHICKEN AND CORN COBB SALAD

NUT-FREE

*Servings: 4 / Prep time: 10 minutes*

A traditional Cobb salad is a type of chopped salad with a mustard-based dressing and nicely arranged ingredients. You can either buy hard-boiled and peeled eggs or cook them yourself. Buying premade rotisserie chicken means this salad comes together in a snap. When you take the salad for lunches, keep the dressing separate until just before you're ready to eat, otherwise your lettuce will get soggy. Store the salad and the dressing in the fridge for up to five days.

1 head romaine
  lettuce, shredded

2 cups chopped boneless and
  skinless rotisserie chicken

1 (8.75-ounce) can sweet
  corn, drained

1 (2.25-ounce) can sliced
  black olives, drained

½ red onion, finely chopped

½ cup crumbled blue cheese

4 hard-boiled eggs, sliced

8 slices bacon, cooked
  and crumbled

Cobb Salad Dressing
  (see recipe page 146)

1. Arrange the lettuce in four lunch containers.

2. Divide the chicken meat, corn, black olives, red onion, blue cheese, eggs, and bacon between four containers, arranging each in its own pile on the lettuce. Do not stir. Cover and refrigerate.

3. Divide the dressing into four smaller containers and refrigerate.

4. Just before eating, pour the dressing on the salad.

> **INGREDIENT TIP:** To hard-boil an egg, put the eggs in a single layer on the bottom of a large pot and cover with an inch of water over the top of the eggs. Turn the burner on high. When the water boils, cover the pot and turn off the heat. Allow the eggs to sit for 14 minutes, covered, and then plunge them into ice water to stop the cooking. They will keep, unpeeled, in the fridge for up to 5 days.

Per Serving: Calories: 564; Total Fat: 39g; Saturated Fat: 10g; Cholesterol: 279mg; Carbohydrates: 18g; Fiber: 4.5g; Protein: 38g

# NAKED BURRITOS

NUT-FREE

*Servings: 4 / Prep time: 10 minutes / Cook time: 11 minutes*

Basically, a naked burrito is a rice bowl that contains the inside of a burrito without the tortillas. It's an easy recipe to make vegetarian (simply eliminate the ground beef and double the amount of black beans), so you can adapt it to your own dietary needs. Use cooked brown rice, either precooked or frozen, to make this a quick meal. Store the rice bowls in the fridge for up to four days, waiting to add the guacamole, sour cream, salsa, and lime juice until just before you serve.

1 pound ground beef

½ red onion, chopped

¼ cup water

1 teaspoon chili powder

½ teaspoon ground cumin

½ teaspoon garlic powder

2 cups cooked brown rice

1 (15-ounce) can black beans, drained

1 bunch scallions, chopped

1 bunch fresh cilantro, chopped

1 tomato, chopped

½ cup grated Pepper Jack cheese

2 limes, halved

Guacamole (page 149)

½ cup sour cream

½ cup prepared salsa

1. In a large skillet, cook the ground beef, crumbling, until it is browned, about 5 minutes.

2. Add the red onion and cook, stirring, until it softens, about 3 minutes more.

3. Add the water, chili powder, cumin, and garlic powder. Simmer until the liquid reduces, about 3 minutes more.

4. Divide the rice evenly between four containers.

5. Add ¼ of the ground beef mixture, ¼ of the black beans, ¼ of the scallions, ¼ of the cilantro, ¼ of the tomato, and ¼ of the cheese to each container. Stir.

6. Squeeze ½ of a lime over each container. Top with the Guacamole, sour cream, and salsa. Cover and refrigerate.

> **INGREDIENT TIP:** If you plan to reheat these in the microwave, then store the scallions, tomato, cilantro, cheese, lime halves, guacamole, sour cream, and salsa in a separate container. Heat the bowl, and then add the vegetables and sauces.

Per Serving: Calories: 724; Total Fat: 39g; Saturated Fat: 14g; Cholesterol: 103mg; Carbohydrates: 58g; Fiber: 14g; Protein: 38g

94

# QUINOA AND BELL PEPPER SALAD

DAIRY-FREE, GLUTEN-FREE, NUT-FREE, VEGAN

*Servings: 4 / Prep time: 10 minutes / Cook time: 10 minutes*

Crisp, colorful bell peppers add flavor and crunch to this simple quinoa salad. You can cook quinoa ahead in large batches and freeze it in 1-cup servings. Thaw before adding to the salad. This will keep in the fridge for five to six days. Don't add the dressing until you're ready to eat the salad.

2 cups cooked quinoa
(see tip below)

1 red bell pepper,
stem, ribs, and seeds
removed, chopped

1 yellow bell pepper,
stem, ribs, and seeds
removed, chopped

1 green bell pepper,
stem, ribs, and seeds
removed, chopped

1 bunch scallions, chopped

Cilantro-Lime Dressing
(see page 150)

1. In a large bowl, combine the quinoa, bell peppers, and scallions. Divide evenly between four containers and refrigerate.

2. Before eating, toss with the dressing.

INGREDIENT TIP: To cook quinoa, rinse it thoroughly in a sieve. This removes bitter flavors from the grain. Then, combine 1 cup of quinoa and 1¾ cups of vegetable broth or water in a pan. Add ½ teaspoon of salt. Bring to a boil over high heat, then lower the heat to medium-low, cover, and cook for 15 minutes or until the liquid is absorbed. Fluff with a fork. This makes 3 cups of cooked quinoa.

Per Serving: Calories: 271; Total Fat: 16g; Saturated Fat: 2g; Cholesterol: 0mg; Carbohydrates: 29g; Fiber: 5g; Protein: 6g

# SWEET POTATO AND SPINACH FRITTATA

GLUTEN-FREE, NUT-FREE, VEGETARIAN

Servings: 4 / Prep time: 15 minutes / Cook time: 15 minutes

Frittatas are super easy meal prep superstars because they refrigerate and freeze well, and they are easy to customize with ingredients you have on hand. You can make this contain animal protein by adding 5 ounces of canned salmon (drained) as you cook your vegetables. Freeze in single-serving slices for up to six months or refrigerate for up to five days. If you're using salmon, refrigerate for up to three days.

3 tablespoons olive oil

1 sweet potato, peeled and grated

½ red onion, chopped

2 cups spinach, chopped

½ teaspoon sea salt

¼ teaspoon freshly cracked black pepper

8 eggs, beaten

¼ cup milk

1 teaspoon Dijon mustard

½ teaspoon garlic powder

¼ cup shredded cheddar cheese

1. Set an oven rack 4 to 6 inches under the broiler. Preheat the broiler to high.

2. In a large ovenproof skillet, heat the olive oil over medium-high heat until it shimmers. Add the sweet potato and red onion and cook without stirring until the sweet potato crisps and browns, about 5 minutes.

3. Stir and add the spinach, salt, and pepper. Cook, stirring, for an additional 2 to 3 minutes, until the spinach is soft.

4. In a large bowl, whisk together the eggs, milk, mustard, and garlic powder.

5. On the heat, arrange the vegetables in a single layer in the bottom of the skillet. Pour the egg mixture over the top of the vegetables, tilting the pan to distribute it evenly.

6. Cook until the eggs set around the edges of the pan. Use a silicone spatula to pull the edges away from the sides of the pan. Tilt the pan to allow uncooked egg to run into the spots where you've pulled the eggs from the edge of the pan.

7. When the eggs have set around the edges again, sprinkle with the cheese. Place under the broiler until the top is puffy and browned, about 3 minutes more.

8. Cut into four wedges and place each wedge into its own container. Refrigerate.

> **SUBSTITUTION TIP:** You can substitute any shredded or crumbled cheese for the cheddar—try ¼ cup of grated Parmesan, crumbled feta, shredded Swiss, or any other cheese of your choice.

Per Serving: Calories: 308; Total Fat: 23g; Saturated Fat: 6g; Cholesterol: 380mg; Carbohydrates: 10g; Fiber: 1.5g; Protein: 16g

# BRUSSELS SPROUTS BUDDHA BOWL

DAIRY-FREE, GLUTEN-FREE, VEGAN

*Servings: 4 / Prep time: 10 minutes / Cook time: 50 minutes*

Roasted Brussels sprouts and shallots bring deep, caramelized flavors to this delicious vegan Buddha bowl. Either buy the rice precooked or cook a large batch on the weekend and save the cooked rice in 1-cup servings in the freezer for up to six months. Store the garlic sauce separately from the Buddha bowl and add it just before you serve. The Buddha bowls will keep in the fridge for up to five days.

2 cups Brussels sprouts, halved

2 tablespoons olive oil

8 shallots, peeled and quartered lengthwise

½ teaspoon sea salt

¼ teaspoon freshly cracked black pepper

2 cups cooked brown rice

1 (15-ounce) can cannellini beans, drained

1 (7-ounce) jar roasted red bell peppers, drained and chopped

Lemon-Garlic Sauce (page 154)

1. Preheat the oven to 400°F.

2. In a large bowl, toss the Brussels sprouts with the olive oil, shallots, salt, and pepper. Mix well.

3. Spread in a single layer on two rimmed baking sheets. Roast in the preheated oven until the Brussels sprouts begin to brown, about 50 minutes. Cool.

4. Divide the cooked brown rice evenly between four containers. Top each with the cooled Brussels sprouts, shallots, cannellini beans, and roasted red bell peppers.

5. Seal and refrigerate. Just before eating, top with the sauce.

---

**SUBSTITUTION TIP:** If you can't find canned cannellini beans, you can substitute canned white beans, great Northern beans, kidney beans, or chickpeas.

---

Per Serving: Calories: 623; Total Fat: 35g; Saturated Fat: 5g; Cholesterol: 0mg; Carbohydrates: 67g; Fiber: 11g; Protein: 14g

98

# RAW VEGAN PAD THAI

DAIRY-FREE, GLUTEN-FREE, VEGAN

*Servings: 4 / Prep time: 10 minutes*

Crisp vegetable "noodles" are the basis of this crunchy and delicious lunch bowl. To make vegetable noodles, either use a spiralizer with the angel-hair attachment, or peel the cucumber into long ribbons using a traditional vegetable peeler, and then use a paring knife to cut them into long fettuccine-size strands. This will keep in the fridge for up to four days. Do not freeze.

4 medium cucumbers, cut into noodles

1 bunch scallions, sliced

1 bunch cilantro, chopped

¼ cup chopped peanuts

3 carrots, grated

1 cup bean sprouts

Juice of 1 lime

Easy Peanut Sauce (page 148)

1. In a large bowl, combine the cucumber noodles, scallions, cilantro, peanuts, carrots, and bean sprouts. Mix with the lime juice.

2. Divide evenly between four containers. Cover and refrigerate.

3. Just before eating, mix with the sauce.

> **RECIPE TIP:** If you'd like to bring some heat to your pad Thai, add up to 1 teaspoon of sriracha. Whisk it with the peanut sauce before adding to the vegetables.

Per Serving: Calories: 364; Total Fat: 22g; Saturated Fat: 3.5g; Cholesterol: 0mg; Carbohydrates: 27g; Fiber: 10g; Protein: 16g

# SPICY SALMON SALAD PITAS

DAIRY-FREE, NUT-FREE

*Servings: 4 / Prep time: 10 minutes*

Pump up the heat as much as you'd like in these delicious salmon salad pitas. If you've got a high tolerance for spice, then feel free to add more sriracha or hot sauce to make it even spicier. The salmon salad will keep for up to four days in the fridge. Do not freeze. Store it separately from the pitas so the bread doesn't get soggy and spoon it in just before you serve it.

2 (5-ounce) cans salmon, drained

Grated zest and juice of ½ an orange, divided

1 fennel bulb, cored and finely chopped

2 tablespoons chopped fresh fennel fronds

½ red onion, finely chopped

½ cup fresh or frozen peas

¼ cup mayonnaise

1 teaspoon sriracha (or another hot sauce of your choice)

½ teaspoon sea salt

4 pitas, halved

1. In a large bowl, combine the salmon, orange juice, fennel bulb and fronds, onion, and peas.

2. In a small bowl, whisk together the mayonnaise, sriracha, salt, and orange zest.

3. Toss the dressing with the salmon salad. Divide it evenly between four containers.

4. Just before eating, spoon the salmon salad into the pitas.

> **SUBSTITUTION TIP:** This recipe works well for tuna, as well. Replace the salmon with water-packed tuna and replace the orange zest and juice with the zest and juice of 1 lemon.

Per Serving: Calories: 373; Total Fat: 13g; Saturated Fat: 2.5g; Cholesterol: 44mg; Carbohydrates: 42g; Fiber: 4g; Protein: 23g

# CLASSIC TUNA MELT

NUT-FREE

*Servings: 2 / Prep time: 10 minutes / Cook time: 5 minutes*

If you like a good tuna melt, this one is easy to make. Choose your favorite whole-grain bread, an English muffin, or even a thick, chewy piece of sourdough. Reheat this ready-made under the broiler for about five minutes, or assemble all the parts, take it to work, and assemble the full sandwich there if you've got a broiler at work. The tuna salad will keep in the fridge for up to five days.

1 (5-ounce) can water-packed tuna, drained

Grated zest and juice of 1 lemon

2 tablespoons chopped fresh dill

1 celery stalk, finely chopped

½ red bell pepper, stems, ribs, and seeds removed, finely chopped

¼ cup mayonnaise

½ teaspoon Dijon mustard

¼ teaspoon sea salt

2 thick-cut slices of bread, toasted

¼ cup grated cheddar cheese

1. In a medium bowl, combine the tuna, lemon zest and juice, dill, celery, and red bell pepper. Add the mayonnaise, mustard, and salt, then mix well.

2. Set an oven rack 4 to 6 inches under the broiler. Set the broiler to high. Place the toasted bread on a rimmed baking sheet.

3. Spoon the tuna mixture onto the two pieces of bread and spread it in an even layer. Sprinkle each with 2 tablespoons of the cheese.

4. Broil until the cheese melts, about 5 minutes.

5. Let cool. Then place each sandwich into a separate container or resealable bag. Refrigerate.

> **SUBSTITUTION TIP:** Replace 2 tablespoons of the mayonnaise with softened herbed cream cheese and mix well in a small bowl with the mayonnaise and mustard. Then, mix with the tuna mixture as written for a slightly gooier, more flavorful sandwich.

Per Serving: Calories: 454; Total Fat: 28g; Saturated Fat: 6.5g; Cholesterol: 67mg; Carbohydrates: 26g; Fiber: 2g; Protein: 24g

# EASY PASTA PRIMAVERA
NUT-FREE, VEGETARIAN

*Servings: 4 / Prep time: 10 minutes / Cook time: 15 minutes*

You can make this easy pasta dish either vegetarian or vegan—to make it vegan, all you need to do is omit the Parmesan cheese. The vegetables add bright colors to this simple vegetarian sauce. Try to cut the vegetables in a uniform size so they'll all cook at roughly the same rate. This will keep in the fridge for up to five days. You can freeze it for up to six months, but it always tastes best when the vegetables are fresh.

¼ cup olive oil

2 carrots, julienned

1 onion, thinly sliced

1 red bell pepper, stem, ribs, and seeds removed, julienned

4 medium zucchini, julienned

1 teaspoon dried Italian seasoning

3 garlic cloves, minced

½ teaspoon sea salt

¼ teaspoon freshly cracked black pepper

8 ounces rotini pasta, cooked according to package directions and drained

10 cherry tomatoes, quartered

¼ cup chopped fresh basil

¼ cup shredded Parmesan cheese (omit for vegan)

1. In a large skillet or pot, heat the olive oil over medium-high heat until it shimmers.

2. Add the carrots, onion, bell pepper, zucchini, and Italian seasoning. Cook, stirring occasionally, until the vegetables are crisp-tender, 5 to 7 minutes.

3. Add the garlic and cook, stirring constantly, for 30 seconds.

4. Add the salt and pepper and stir. Remove from the heat.

5. Toss with the warm pasta, tomatoes, and basil. Sprinkle with the Parmesan cheese. Let cool.

6. Divide evenly between four containers. Refrigerate.

> **SUBSTITUTION TIP:** If you are vegan but prefer your pasta with a cheesy taste, add up to ¼ cup of nutritional yeast in place of the Parmesan. For crunch, add up to ¼ cup of chopped walnuts or pine nuts when you add the tomatoes and basil.

Per Serving: Calories: 437; Total Fat: 17g; Saturated Fat: 3g; Cholesterol: 4mg; Carbohydrates: 59g; Fiber: 7g; Protein: 13g

# ALMOND-CRUSTED HALIBUT

DAIRY-FREE

*Servings: 4 / Prep time: 10 minutes / Cook time: 20 minutes*

The savory coating of almonds and bread crumbs is flavored with herbs to add texture to sweet halibut. If you don't have or can't find halibut, substitute any other white-fleshed fish, such as cod or haddock. This will keep in the fridge for up to three days. Do not freeze.

4 (4-ounce) halibut fillets, pin bones removed

2 teaspoons Dijon mustard

¼ cup almond meal (almond flour)

¼ cup panko bread crumbs (or make your own)

1 teaspoon dried thyme

½ teaspoon garlic powder

Grated zest of ½ an orange

3 tablespoons olive oil

½ teaspoon sea salt

¼ teaspoon freshly cracked black pepper

¼ cup chopped fresh Italian parsley

1. Preheat the oven to 450°F.

2. Place the halibut fillets, skin-side down, on a rimmed baking sheet. Spread each with ½ teaspoon of Dijon mustard.

3. In a small bowl, combine the almond meal, bread crumbs, thyme, garlic powder, orange zest, olive oil, salt, pepper, and parsley. Mix well.

4. Sprinkle the almond meal mixture liberally on the mustard-coated halibut, pressing in the coating to compress.

5. Bake in the oven until the almond mixture is golden and the halibut is opaque, about 20 minutes.

6. Remove from oven and let cool. Once cool, place each fillet in its own container. Refrigerate.

> **SUBSTITUTION TIP:** Make this gluten-free by omitting the bread crumbs and replacing them with an additional ½ cup of ground almond meal.

Per Serving: Calories: 248; Total Fat: 15g; Saturated Fat: 2g; Cholesterol: 51mg; Carbohydrates: 6g; Fiber: 1g; Protein: 21g

# CUCUMBER, SHIITAKE, AND BROCCOLINI LETTUCE ROLLS

DAIRY-FREE, VEGETARIAN

*Servings: 2 / Prep time: 20 minutes / Cook time: 15 minutes*

These seasoned lettuce rolls are a great way to lunch. With deep flavors of sesame oil and a delicious peanut dipping sauce, the rolls are the perfect crunchy vegetarian meal. They don't freeze well, however, so make only as many as you plan to eat in a few days and store them in the fridge for up to four days.

2 tablespoons olive oil

2 cups sliced
   shiitake mushrooms

2 cups broccolini

1 teaspoon freshly grated
   ginger root

2 garlic cloves, minced

½ teaspoon sesame oil

1 teaspoon reduced-sodium
   soy sauce

Juice of 1 lime

1 cup cooked brown
   rice, cooled

½ cup chopped peanuts

8 pieces butter lettuce

Easy Peanut Sauce (page 148)

1. In a large skillet, heat the olive oil over medium-high heat until it shimmers.

2. Add the shiitake mushrooms, broccolini, and ginger. Cook, stirring occasionally, until the vegetables begin to brown, about 5 minutes.

3. Add the garlic cloves and cook, stirring constantly, for 30 seconds.

4. Add the sesame oil, soy sauce, and lime juice. Cook, stirring occasionally, until the liquid is evaporated, about 3 minutes more. Cool.

5. In a large bowl, combine the cooled vegetable mixture, cooked brown rice, and peanuts. Mix well.

6. Spoon onto the 8 lettuce leaves and form into rolls.

7. Place 4 rolls each in two containers. Refrigerate.

8. To serve, dip in the peanut sauce.

> **DIETARY SWAP:** If you'd like to have some animal protein with this, add ½ cup cooked baby shrimp in step 5.

Per Serving: Calories: 764; Total Fat: 52g; Saturated Fat: 8g; Cholesterol: 0mg; Carbohydrates: 55g; Fiber: 12g; Protein: 26g

# ZOODLES WITH TURKEY RAGU

DAIRY-FREE, GLUTEN-FREE, NUT-FREE

*Servings: 4 / Prep time: 20 minutes / Cook time: 20 minutes*

Zoodles are super easy to make—simply use a spiralizer to cut zucchini into noodles, buy them in the grocery store precut, or make them using a vegetable peeler to create long strips of zucchini that you then cut in half to make fettuccine-style noodles. They're the perfect noodle substitute for folks counting carbs or wishing to avoid gluten. They'll store in the fridge for up to five days or the freezer for up to six months.

2 tablespoons olive oil

1 pound ground turkey

1 onion, finely chopped

1 (15-ounce) can crushed tomatoes and basil, undrained

1 teaspoon garlic powder

1 tablespoon dried Italian seasoning

½ teaspoon sea salt

¼ teaspoon freshly cracked black pepper

Pinch red pepper flakes

4 medium zucchini, cut into noodles (about 4 cups of zoodles)

1. In a large skillet, heat the olive oil over medium-high heat until it shimmers.

2. Add the turkey and cook, crumbling, until browned, about 5 minutes.

3. Remove the turkey from the pan with a slotted spoon, leaving the oil in the pan.

4. Cook the onion, stirring occasionally, until soft, about 5 minutes.

5. Return the turkey to the pan. Add the crushed tomatoes and basil, garlic powder, Italian seasoning, salt, pepper, and red pepper flakes. Bring to a simmer. Reduce the heat to medium-low. Cook, stirring occasionally, for 5 minutes.

6. Add the zoodles. Cook, stirring occasionally, for 5 minutes more. Remove from heat and let cool.

7. Divide evenly between two containers. Refrigerate.

> **INGREDIENT TIP:** There's no need to peel the zucchini before making the zoodles. Cooking tenderizes the peel and leaving it on adds fiber and a nice green color.

Per Serving: Calories: 309; Total Fat: 16g; Saturated Fat: 3g; Cholesterol: 76mg; Carbohydrates: 17g; Fiber: 5g; Protein: 27g

# CREAMY CHICKEN QUESADILLAS
NUT-FREE

*Servings: 4 / Prep time: 15 minutes / Cook time: 15 minutes*

If you like jalapeño poppers, then you'll enjoy these creamy chicken and jala-peño quesadillas, which have similar ingredients to jalapeño poppers but in a different form. Use cooked chicken from a store-bought rotisserie chicken (minus the skin and bones) or use leftover chicken. For an extra-special treat, enjoy the quesadillas spread with premade jalapeño jelly. Alternatively, enjoy them with some fresh Guacamole (page 149) for dipping. These will keep in the fridge for up to five days.

8 (12-inch) flour tortillas

½ cup cream cheese, softened

1 cup cooked boneless, skinless chicken

1 (4-ounce) can chopped diced jalapeños

¼ cup chopped scallions

½ cup shredded Pepper Jack cheese

¼ cup olive oil

1. Preheat the oven to 425°F.

2. Place 4 flour tortillas on two rimmed baking sheets. Spread 2 tablespoons of cream cheese on each tortilla.

3. Sprinkle each tortilla with ¼ cup of the cooked chicken, ¼ of the jalapeños, and 1 tablespoon of the scallions.

4. Sprinkle each with 2 tablespoons of cheese and top with one of the remaining tortillas.

5. Bake in the preheated oven for 15 minutes, until golden brown.

6. Cut each into 4 wedges. Place 4 wedges into each of four containers. Refrigerate.

> **SUBSTITUTION TIP:** Make these gluten-free by replac-ing the flour tortillas with corn tortillas.

Per Serving: Calories: 962; Total Fat: 44g; Saturated Fat: 17g; Cholesterol: 72mg; Carbohydrates: 109g; Fiber: 4g; Protein: 30g

# BARBECUE CHICKEN PIZZA

NUT-FREE

*Servings:* 4 / *Prep time:* 15 minutes / *Cook time:* 15 minutes per pizza

You'll need to cook each of these pizzas separately—one pizza makes two servings. If you have a baking stone, use it. Otherwise, simply heat a baking sheet in the oven while you prepare the crust, so it is nice and hot when you put the pizza on it. This will keep in the fridge for up to five days or in the freezer for up to six months. Cut into wedges before freezing.

1½ cups flour, plus more to prevent sticking

1 teaspoon baking powder

½ teaspoon sea salt

½ cup very cold water

1½ tablespoons olive oil, plus additional to grease the grill

½ cup Sweet and Spicy Barbecue Sauce (page 147)

2 cups cooked chopped boneless and skinless chicken

½ red onion, finely chopped

1 cup shredded mozzarella cheese

1. Preheat the oven to 400°F with a baking stone or a rimmed baking sheet in the oven.

2. In a bowl, combine the flour, baking powder, and sea salt.

3. Mix in the water and olive oil. Form into two balls. Sprinkle a bit of additional flour on your work surface and roll out each ball to ½-inch thickness.

4. Spread the dough with ¼ cup each of the barbecue sauce.

5. Sprinkle each with 1 cup of the chicken and divide the red onion evenly across both pizzas. Sprinkle each with ½ cup of cheese.

6. Working one pizza at a time, bake on the hot stone or baking sheet until the crust is golden and the cheese bubbly, about 15 minutes per pizza.

7. Slice into four pieces and refrigerate each piece in its own container.

> **COOKING TIP:** To transfer each pizza to the hot baking stone or pan, use two large spatulas or a baking peel.

Per Serving: Calories: 486; Total Fat: 20g; Saturated Fat: 6.5g; Cholesterol: 75mg; Carbohydrates: 46g; Fiber: 2g; Protein: 30g

# CHICKEN AND BLACK BEAN TACO SALAD

GLUTEN-FREE, NUT-FREE

*Servings: 4 / Prep time: 10 minutes / Cook time: 15 minutes*

One of the things that makes taco salad such a tasty lunch is how easy it is to customize it to your own personal tastes. This version has all the fixings—chicken, shredded cheese, beans, and olives—but feel free to replace ingredients with your favorite proteins, toppings, or vegetables. Store the salad separately from the guacamole and salsa and add those just before serving. The salad will keep in the fridge for up to five days.

2 tablespoons olive oil

1 pound boneless, skinless chicken breast, cut into 1-inch pieces

¼ cup water

1 teaspoon onion powder

½ teaspoon garlic powder

½ teaspoon ground cumin

1 teaspoon chili powder

½ teaspoon sea salt

8 cups shredded iceberg lettuce

1 (15-ounce) can black beans, drained

1 bunch scallions, chopped

1 (3.8-ounce) can sliced black olives, drained

1 cup chopped tomato

¼ cup chopped fresh cilantro

½ cup shredded Pepper Jack cheese

Guacamole (see page 149)

½ cup ready-made salsa

1. In a large skillet, heat the olive oil over medium-high heat until it shimmers.

2. Add the chicken breast and cook, stirring occasionally, until the chicken is browned, 5 to 7 minutes.

3. Add the water, onion powder, garlic powder, cumin, chili powder, and salt. Bring to a simmer and reduce heat to low, stirring. Cook until the chicken is coated, and the liquid is reduced by half, about 3 minutes more. Cool.

4. In a large bowl, combine the lettuce, black beans, cooled chicken, olives, tomato, cilantro, and cheese. Toss to mix. Divide evenly between four containers and refrigerate.

5. To serve, toss with the Guacamole and salsa.

> **INGREDIENT TIP:** Want something crunchy? Add up to ¼ cup of crushed tortilla chips to each serving just before eating.

Per Serving: Calories: 551; Total Fat: 30g; Saturated Fat: 5.5g; Cholesterol: 95mg; Carbohydrates: 36g; Fiber: 14g; Protein: 39g

# SWEET POTATO AND BROWN RICE SALAD

DAIRY-FREE, GLUTEN-FREE, NUT-FREE, VEGAN

*Servings: 4 / Prep time: 10 minutes / Cook time: 1 hour*

This vegan salad comes together in about 1 hour—but most of that is inactive time spent baking your sweet potatoes and cooking your rice. You can always bake sweet potatoes and cook the rice in big batches and then freeze them in single-serving containers in the freezer for quick use in recipes. You'll love the sweet, earthy flavors of the potatoes along with the veggies and the Lemon-Dijon Vinaigrette that adds tremendous flavor to this salad. The salad will keep in the fridge for up to five days or the freezer for up to six months.

2 sweet potatoes, pricked with a fork

½ cup cooked brown rice

1 red bell pepper, stem, ribs, and seeds removed, chopped

1 bunch scallions, chopped

1 (15-ounce) can chickpeas, drained

1 bunch Italian parsley, chopped

Lemon-Dijon Vinaigrette (page 152)

1. Preheat the oven to 425°F.

2. Bake the sweet potatoes on a baking sheet until they are fork-tender, about 55 minutes. Cool.

3. Chop the cooked sweet potatoes. Put them in a bowl with the brown rice, red bell pepper, scallions, chickpeas, and parsley.

4. Divide evenly between four containers and refrigerate. Just before eating, toss with the vinaigrette.

> **DIETARY SWAP:** If you'd like to add some animal protein to this salad, replace the chickpeas with 2 cups of cooked chicken with the bones and skin removed.

Per Serving: Calories: 338; Total Fat: 16g; Saturated Fat: 2g; Cholesterol: 0mg; Carbohydrates: 42g; Fiber: 9g; Protein: 8g

# ROASTED BEET AND FETA MASON JAR SALADS

GLUTEN-FREE, NUT-FREE, VEGETARIAN

*Servings: 4 / Prep time: 10 minutes / Cook time: 1 hour*

Roasting the beets brings out their deep, sweet, earthy flavors, making them the perfect, flavorful, colorful ingredient to build a tasty mason jar salad. Pepitas (hulled pumpkin seeds) add crunch, while feta adds a salty tang. These will keep in the fridge for up to five days, but don't freeze them.

12 beets, trimmed, peeled, and cut into ½-inch pieces

3 tablespoons olive oil

½ teaspoon sea salt

¼ teaspoon freshly cracked black pepper

½ cup feta cheese

½ cup pepitas

4 scallions, thinly sliced

Lemon-Dijon Vinaigrette (page 152)

1. Preheat the oven to 450°F.

2. In a bowl, toss the beets with the olive oil, salt, and pepper.

3. Spread the beets in a single layer on two rimmed baking sheets and bake in the preheated oven until they are soft and browning, about 55 minutes. Cool completely.

4. Spoon the beets evenly into four large mason jars.

5. Sprinkle each with 2 tablespoons of feta, 2 tablespoons of pepitas, and ¼ of the scallions. Cover and refrigerate.

6. Add the dressing to the jar and shake just before eating.

> **SUBSTITUTION TIP:** Not a fan of beets? Any root vegetable will work here—you'll need about 4 cups of cooked root vegetable, so a butternut squash or 3 to 4 sweet potatoes would also work in place of the beets.

Per Serving: Calories: 514; Total Fat: 35g; Saturated Fat: 7.5g; Cholesterol: 10mg; Carbohydrates: 30g; Fiber: 8.5g; Protein: 17g

# FETA, ASPARAGUS, AND RED POTATO SALAD

GLUTEN-FREE, NUT-FREE, VEGETARIAN

*Servings: 4 / Prep time: 10 minutes / Cook time: 1 hour*

You can cook the asparagus and red potato at the same time—simply put them on separate rimmed baking sheets and put the asparagus in the oven when the potatoes have 15 to 20 minutes remaining in cooking. This salad will keep in the fridge for up to five days.

2 pounds red potatoes, cut into 1-inch pieces

3 tablespoons olive oil, divided

1 teaspoon sea salt, divided

¼ teaspoon freshly cracked black pepper, divided

1 bunch asparagus spears, trimmed and chopped

½ cup feta cheese

½ red onion, finely chopped

Lemon-Garlic Sauce (page 154)

1. Preheat the oven to 400°F.

2. In one bowl, toss the potatoes with 2 tablespoons of the olive oil, ½ teaspoon of the salt, and ⅛ teaspoon of the pepper.

3. In another bowl, toss the asparagus with the remaining 1 tablespoon of olive oil, the remaining ½ teaspoon of the salt, and the remaining ⅛ teaspoon of the pepper.

4. Spread the potatoes and the asparagus on two separate rimmed baking sheets.

5. Bake the potatoes in the preheated oven for 50 to 60 minutes (until soft), stirring once. Cool.

6. After about 40 minutes, put the asparagus in the preheated oven and roast until it begins to brown, 10 to 15 minutes. Cool.

7. In a large bowl, toss the cooled potatoes and asparagus, feta cheese, red onion, and the sauce. Separate into four containers and refrigerate.

> **INGREDIENT TIP:** To trim asparagus, using both hands, hold each spear about ½ inch from each end. Bend the spear slightly. It will snap where it should be trimmed. Throw away the tough end and chop the remaining spear into ½-inch pieces.

Per Serving: Calories: 589; Total Fat: 41g; Saturated Fat: 7g; Cholesterol: 10mg; Carbohydrates: 44g; Fiber: 5.5g; Protein: 11g

# ROASTED ROOT VEGETABLE CHOPPED SALAD

GLUTEN-FREE, DAIRY-FREE, NUT-FREE, VEGETARIAN

*Servings: 4 / Prep time: 10 minutes / Cook time: 1 hour*

When you roast root vegetables, they develop deep, caramelized flavors that make them an irresistible salad ingredient. Adding some chopped fresh herbs brings bright, fresh flavors that balance the flavors of the vegetables, while Honey Mustard Dressing brings sweetness and a hint of acidity to the dish for a well-balanced flavor profile. This will keep in the fridge for up to five days.

1 bulb celeriac, peeled and cut into 1-inch pieces

1 fennel bulb, cored and cut into 1-inch pieces

4 carrots, cut into 1-inch pieces

2 sweet potatoes, cut into 1-inch pieces

8 shallots, peeled and quartered

¼ cup olive oil

1 teaspoon dried thyme

½ teaspoon sea salt

¼ teaspoon freshly cracked black pepper

2 tablespoons chopped fennel fronds

Honey Mustard Dressing (page 151)

1. Preheat the oven to 425°F.

2. In a large bowl, toss the celeriac, fennel, carrots, sweet potatoes, shallots, olive oil, thyme, salt, and pepper. Spread in an even layer on two rimmed baking sheets.

3. Bake in the preheated oven until the vegetables are soft and beginning to brown, about 1 hour. Cool.

4. Divide evenly into four containers. Sprinkle each with the fennel fronds. Seal and refrigerate.

5. Just before eating, toss with the dressing.

> **SUBSTITUTION TIP:** While homemade is always best, you can also substitute any store-bought salad dressing—each serving will require two tablespoons of dressing.

Per Serving: Calories: 491; Total Fat: 28g; Saturated Fat: 4g; Cholesterol: 0mg; Carbohydrates: 58g; Fiber: 10g; Protein: 6g

# CHICKEN, MANGO, AND QUINOA BOWL

GLUTEN-FREE, DAIRY-FREE

*Servings: 4 / Prep time: 10 minutes / Cook time: 15 minutes*

It's always a good idea when you're doing meal prep to fill your freezer full of single servings of cooked grains such as quinoa and brown rice, as well as cooked and chopped animal proteins such as chicken or turkey. That way, when you're ready to meal prep on a super busy Sunday, you can thaw instead of taking the time to roast and simmer. So, while this recipe calls for cooking the quinoa at the time, if you've got cooked quinoa in the freezer, then you'll need 2 cups of cooked quinoa to make the four servings for this recipe. It will keep in the fridge for up to five days.

1⅓ cups water

⅔ cup quinoa

½ teaspoon sea salt

2 cups rotisserie chicken meat, boneless and skinless, chopped

1 mango, peeled and cut into ½-inch cubes

½ red onion, finely chopped

¼ cup chopped fresh cilantro

½ cup chopped peanuts

Easy Peanut Sauce (page 148)

1. In a pot, bring the water, quinoa, and salt to a simmer over medium-high heat. Reduce the heat to medium-low and cook, uncovered, until the water is absorbed, about 5 minutes.

2. Remove from the heat, cover, and allow to rest for 5 minutes. Fluff with a fork. Cool completely.

3. In a large bowl, combine the cooled quinoa, the chicken, mango, red onion, cilantro, and peanuts. Mix well. Spoon evenly into four containers and refrigerate.

4. Before eating, drizzle with the sauce.

113

> **SUBSTITUTION TIP:** If you have a peanut allergy, you can use cashews or almonds in place of the peanuts in the salad, and almond or cashew butter in place of the peanut butter in the peanut sauce.

Per Serving: Calories: 499; Total Fat: 25g; Saturated Fat: 4.5g; Cholesterol: 60mg; Carbohydrates: 40g; Fiber: 6.5g; Protein: 32g

# TERIYAKI SALMON BOWL

DAIRY-FREE, NUT-FREE

*Servings:* 4 / *Prep time:* 10 minutes / *Cook time:* 15 minutes

Teriyaki glaze is super easy to make, and it keeps well in the fridge or freezer, so you can double or triple the batch of sauce and save more for later. It's great on chicken, fish, vegetables, or grains, meaning it's a great all-purpose sauce to have on hand. These teriyaki bowls will keep in the fridge for four to five days.

1 cup plus 2 tablespoons of water, divided

¼ cup soy sauce

¼ cup packed brown sugar

½ teaspoon ground ginger

½ teaspoon garlic powder

2 tablespoons cornstarch

2 tablespoons olive oil

4 (4-ounce) salmon fillets

2 cups cooked brown rice

1 (8-ounce) can pineapple chunks in juice, drained

4 scallions, thinly sliced

1. In a pot, combine 1 cup of the water, soy sauce, brown sugar, ground ginger, and garlic powder. Bring to a simmer over medium-high heat. Simmer, whisking, until the sugar is completely dissolved.

2. In a small bowl, whisk together the cornstarch and the remaining 2 tablespoons of water. Whisk into the simmering sauce. Continue to simmer, whisking, until the sauce thickens, about 2 minutes. Remove from the heat and cool completely. Divide into two equal parts in separate bowls.

3. Preheat a grill or grill pan over medium-high heat and brush it with the olive oil. Brush the flesh side of the salmon with one of the bowls of the teriyaki sauce (discard any leftover sauce used to brush the salmon). Grill until the salmon is opaque, 5 to 7 minutes per side. Remove from heat and let cool.

4. Fill four containers with ½ cup each of the cooked rice. Add the pineapples and stir. Then add the salmon and drizzle with the remaining teriyaki sauce. Sprinkle with the scallions.

> **DIETARY SWAP:** You can make these bowls vegan by replacing the salmon with 12 ounces of extra-firm tofu. Cut the tofu into 1-inch pieces, toss with half the teriyaki sauce, and bake them in a 450°F oven for about 30 minutes.

Per Serving: Calories: 424; Total Fat: 9g; Saturated Fat: 1.5g; Cholesterol: 72mg; Carbohydrates: 54g; Fiber: 2.5g; Protein: 30g

# STEAK AND BLUE CHEESE COBB SALAD

GLUTEN-FREE, NUT-FREE

*Servings: 4 / Prep time: 10 minutes / Cook time: 10 minutes*

Skirt steak works well in Cobb salads—it cooks quickly and is very tender when you cut it against the grain. Marinate the steak for at least three hours to give it a great, garlicky flavor that goes well with the rest of the delicious salad. Don't add the dressing until just before you eat it. This salad will keep in the fridge for up to five days.

6 garlic cloves, minced

¼ cup chopped fresh Italian parsley

¾ cup balsamic vinegar or red wine vinegar

¼ cup plus 2 tablespoons olive oil, divided

1 shallot, peeled and finely chopped

1 teaspoon Dijon mustard

1 teaspoon Worcestershire sauce

1 pound skirt steak

8 cups shredded romaine lettuce

½ red onion, finely chopped

1 cup finely chopped tomatoes

4 hard-boiled eggs, peeled and sliced

½ cup crumbled blue cheese

8 slices bacon, cooked and crumbled

Cobb Salad Dressing (page 146)

1. In a bowl, combine the garlic, parsley, vinegar, ¼ cup of the oil, shallot, mustard, and Worcestershire sauce. Whisk well.

2. Pour into a large zipper bag with the skirt steak. Seal and massage the bag to distribute the marinade. Refrigerate and marinate for at least 3 hours and up to 12 hours.

3. Preheat the remaining 2 tablespoons of olive oil in a large skillet over medium-high heat until it shimmers.

4. Remove the steak from the marinade and pat it dry with paper towels.

5. Cook it in the preheated skillet until it reaches an internal temperature of 145°F, 3 to 4 minutes per side.

6. Cool the steak. When it is cool, slice it into ¼- to ½-inch thick pieces against the grain.

7. Divide the lettuce, onion, tomatoes, eggs, blue cheese, bacon, and cooled steak among four containers. Refrigerate.

8. Drizzle with the Cobb Salad Dressing before eating.

Per Serving: Calories: 590; Total Fat: 44g; Saturated Fat: 12g; Cholesterol: 276mg; Carbohydrates: 12g; Fiber: 3g; Protein: 37g

# SPINACH, FETA, AND TURKEY GRILLED CHEESE

NUT-FREE

*Servings: 2 / Prep time: 10 minutes / Cook time: 10 minutes*

Grilled cheese sandwiches are the ultimate comfort food—the gooey, melted cheese made them a childhood favorite for many of us. This is a grown-up version, but it's still delicious. If possible, assemble the sandwiches but don't cook them until lunchtime (you can even use a tabletop grill or panini press to make them). Otherwise, go ahead and make them in advance and enjoy them cooled. They're still delicious, and they'll keep for about five days in the fridge.

4 slices whole-grain bread

6 ounces deli turkey slices

1 cup baby spinach

½ cup crumbled feta cheese

2 tablespoons melted butter

1. Preheat a panini press, tabletop grill, or a nonstick skillet on medium-high heat.

2. On two pieces of bread, arrange the turkey slices and spinach. Top with the feta and a second piece of bread.

3. Brush the outside of each piece of bread with butter. Cook in your preheated pan or appliance until the bread is golden and the cheese melts, 3 to 4 minutes per side. Remove from heat and let cool.

4. Place each sandwich in a separate container or resealable bag. Refrigerate.

> **INGREDIENT TIP:** Want to add some extra flavor to these sandwiches? Spread the inside of the bottom piece of bread with Dijon mustard. When you melt the butter, add ¼ teaspoon of truffle salt (or another flavored salt you enjoy) before brushing it on the sandwiches.

Per Serving: Calories: 520; Total Fat: 20g; Saturated Fat: 11g; Cholesterol: 81mg; Carbohydrates: 37g; Fiber: 4.5g; Protein: 39g

# STEAK FAJITA BOWLS

DAIRY-FREE, GLUTEN-FREE, NUT-FREE

*Servings: 4 / Prep time: 10 minutes / Cook time: 10 minutes*

Fajitas are an easy choice for lunch prep, and it's super easy to switch out the protein with chicken or shrimp; simply marinate it in the same marinade as you would for the beef and cook it in the hot pan until cooked through—three to five minutes for shrimp, five to seven minutes for chicken.

1 bunch scallions, chopped

3 garlic cloves, minced

1 bunch cilantro, chopped

1 jalapeño, stem, seeds, and ribs removed, minced

Grated zest of 1 lime and juice of 3 limes

¼ cup plus 2 tablespoons olive oil, divided

½ teaspoon sea salt

1 pound skirt steak, cut into 1-inch strips

1 green bell pepper, stem, seeds, and ribs removed and sliced

1 red bell pepper, stem, seeds, and ribs removed and sliced

1 red onion, thinly sliced

2 cups cooked brown rice

Guacamole (page 149)

1. In a blender or food processor, combine the scallions, garlic, cilantro, jalapeño, lime zest and juice, ¼ cup of the olive oil, and the salt. Pulse 10 to 20 times, until it resembles pesto.

2. Set aside 1 tablespoon of the mixture in a small bowl and refrigerate. Add the remaining mixture to a large bowl with the skirt steak, stirring to coat the steak. Refrigerate for at least 3 hours.

3. In a large skillet, heat the remaining 2 tablespoons of olive oil on medium-high. Remove the steak from the marinade and pat away excess with paper towels.

4. Cook the steak, stirring in the hot oil until the steak is cooked through, about 5 minutes.

5. Remove the steak from the fat in the pan with tongs and set it aside. Add the green and red bell peppers and onion to the hot pan and cook, stirring occasionally, until soft, about 5 minutes more.

6. Return the steak to the pan along with the reserved marinade. Cook, stirring, for 1 minute. Cool.

7. Divide the rice, steak, and vegetables evenly between four containers. Refrigerate.

8. Just before eating, spoon the Guacamole on top of the food in the containers.

Per Serving: Calories: 582; Total Fat: 36g; Saturated Fat: 9g; Cholesterol: 74mg; Carbohydrates: 40g; Fiber: 8g; Protein: 28g

# SAUSAGE AND EGG SALAD SANDWICH

DAIRY-FREE, NUT-FREE

*Servings: 2 / Prep time: 10 minutes / Cook time: 7 minutes*

Egg salad sandwiches are a lunch mainstay, but when you add sausage to the mix, they just seem a little more special. Make the egg salad with sausage ahead of time and store it in the fridge for up to five days (it won't freeze well). Spread it on your bread just before eating it—it's a super way to make a tasty meal prep sandwich that won't be soggy when you're ready to eat it.

4 ounces breakfast sausage

4 hard-boiled eggs, peeled and chopped

¼ red onion, finely chopped

¼ red bell pepper, stem, ribs, and seeds removed and finely chopped

2 tablespoons chopped fresh chives

¼ cup mayonnaise or plain Greek yogurt

1 teaspoon Dijon mustard

¼ teaspoon sea salt

⅛ teaspoon freshly cracked black pepper

4 slices whole-grain bread (toasted if you wish)

1. In a medium skillet, cook the breakfast sausage over medium-high heat until it is well-browned, 5 to 7 minutes. Crumble or chop the sausage and allow it to cool.

2. In a large bowl, combine the cooled sausage, the chopped eggs, the onion, bell pepper, and chives. Mix well.

3. Add mayonnaise or yogurt, mustard, salt, and pepper. Mix well.

4. Divide mixture evenly between two containers and refrigerate. Place bread slices into a sandwich bag and set aside.

5. To eat, spoon the egg salad on one slice of bread and cover it with the other. Repeat this process the following day.

> **DIETARY SWAP:** If you're avoiding gluten or carbs, take two or three large pieces of butter lettuce instead of bread and make egg salad lettuce wraps instead.

Per Serving: Calories: 662; Total Fat: 44g; Saturated Fat: 10g; Cholesterol: 420mg; Carbohydrates: 38g; Fiber: 4.5g; Protein: 31g

# SAUSAGE AND SWISS CHARD PENNE

NUT-FREE

*Servings: 4 / Prep time: 10 minutes / Cook time: 20 minutes*

This pasta is delicious either reheated or even chilled. If you can find it, bulk Italian sausage is your best bet. But if you can only find whole Italian sausages, use a sharp paring knife to cut away the casing and use just the sausage inside, discarding the casing. This will keep in the fridge for up to five days, and it freezes well for up to six months.

1 pound bulk Italian sausage

1 onion, chopped

1 red bell pepper, stem, ribs, and seeds removed, chopped

1 bunch Swiss chard, stemmed and chopped

4 garlic cloves, minced

½ cup dry white wine

Grated zest and juice of 1 lemon

1 tablespoon dried Italian seasoning

½ teaspoon sea salt

¼ teaspoon freshly cracked black pepper

Pinch red pepper flakes

16 cherry tomatoes, halved

8 ounces penne pasta, cooked according to package instructions and drained

¼ cup shredded Parmesan cheese

1. In a large skillet, cook the Italian sausage over medium-high heat, crumbling, until browned, 5 to 7 minutes.

2. Remove the sausage from the fat in the pan with a slotted spoon, setting it aside.

3. In the hot pan with the oil from the sausage, add the onion, bell pepper, and Swiss chard. Cook, stirring occasionally, until the vegetables are soft, about 5 minutes. Add the garlic and cook, stirring constantly, for 30 seconds. Return the sausage to the pan.

4. Add the wine, scraping any browned bits from the bottom of the pan with the side of a spoon. Add the lemon zest and juice, Italian seasoning, salt, pepper, and red pepper flakes.

5. Bring to a simmer. Cook, stirring occasionally, until the liquid is reduced by half, 3 to 4 minutes.

6. Add the tomatoes and penne. Cook, stirring, for 3 minutes more. Remove from heat and let cool. Toss with the cheese.

Per Serving: Calories: 520; Total Fat: 13g; Saturated Fat: 4.5g; Cholesterol: 38mg; Carbohydrates: 66g; Fiber: 8.5g; Protein: 33g

# SAUSAGE AND KALE MINI CRUSTLESS QUICHES

GLUTEN-FREE, NUT-FREE

*Servings: 3 / Prep time: 10 minutes / Cook time: 45 minutes*

These mini crustless quiches are a perfect prep meal, and they're delicious for breakfast, lunch, or dinner, so they serve all your prep needs. They also freeze extremely well (up to six months), so doubling or tripling the batch is always an option, and you can refrigerate them for up to five days. Serving size is two mini quiches.

½ pound bulk breakfast sausage

1 red onion, chopped

1 green bell pepper, stem, ribs, and seeds removed, chopped

1 bunch kale, stemmed and chopped

6 eggs, beaten

½ teaspoon Dijon mustard

½ teaspoon garlic powder

1 tablespoon chopped fresh chives

½ teaspoon sea salt

¼ teaspoon freshly cracked black pepper

½ cup shredded cheddar

1. Preheat the oven to 350°F. Grease a six-cup nonstick muffin tin.

2. In a large skillet, cook the breakfast sausage over medium-high heat, crumbling it with a wooden spoon, until browned, 5 to 7 minutes.

3. Remove the sausage from the fat in the pan with a slotted spoon, setting it aside. Let the sausage cool completely.

4. In the hot pan with the oil from the sausage, add the red onion, bell pepper, and kale. Cook, stirring occasionally, until the vegetables are soft, about 5 minutes. Cool completely.

5. In a large bowl, whisk together the eggs, mustard, garlic powder, chives, salt, and pepper. Fold in the cooled sausage, vegetables, and cheese.

6. Spoon into the prepared muffin tins. Bake in the pre-heated oven until the eggs set, about 30 minutes.

7. Let cool and divide evenly between three containers.

Per Serving: Calories: 542; Total Fat: 38g; Saturated Fat: 13g; Cholesterol: 455mg; Carbohydrates: 17g; Fiber: 5g; Protein: 36g

# CHILE-LIME SHRIMP FAJITAS

NUT-FREE

*Servings: 3 / Prep time: 10 minutes / Cook time: 10 minutes*

Do you like spicy food? Then you'll love these shrimp fajitas, which have plenty of heat from a chile pepper. Prepare the shrimp and veggies and refrigerate them for up to three days or freeze them for up to six months. Assemble at the last minute by adding flour tortillas, shredded cheese, and Guacamole.

1 habanero chile, stem, seeds, and ribs removed, finely chopped

Grated zest of 1 lime and juice of 2 limes

2 garlic cloves, minced

¼ cup plus 2 tablespoons olive oil, divided

¼ teaspoon cayenne (or to taste)

1 bunch scallions, chopped

1 bunch cilantro, chopped

1 pound shrimp, peeled, deveined, and tails removed

1 onion, halved, and sliced

2 jalapeño chiles, stem, ribs, and seeds removed, thinly sliced lengthwise

1 green bell pepper, stem, ribs, and seeds removed, thinly sliced

2 carrots, thinly sliced

½ cup shredded Monterey Jack cheese

Guacamole (page 149)

4 fajita-size flour tortillas

1. In a blender or food processor, combine the habanero, lime zest and juice, garlic, ¼ cup of the olive oil, cayenne, scallions, and cilantro. Pulse 10 to 20 times, until it resembles pesto.

2. Set aside 1 tablespoon of the marinade. In a medium bowl, mix the rest of the marinade with the shrimp. Refrigerate for 30 minutes.

3. Remove the shrimp from the marinade and pat dry with paper towels.

4. In a large skillet, heat the remaining 2 tablespoons of olive oil over medium-high heat until it shimmers.

5. Add the onion, jalapeño, bell pepper, and carrots. Cook, stirring occasionally, until the vegetables soften, about 5 minutes.

6. Add the shrimp. Cook, stirring, until the shrimp is pink, about 4 minutes more.

7. Add the reserved marinade. Cook, stirring, for 1 minute more. Remove from heat, let cool, and refrigerate.

8. Divide fajitas evenly between three containers and refrigerate. When ready to eat, serve with tortillas, guacamole, and Monterey Jack cheese, if desired.

Per Serving: Calories: 651; Total Fat: 38g; Saturated Fat: 8.5g; Cholesterol: 260mg; Carbohydrates: 41g; Fiber: 10g; Protein: 42g

# SHRIMP AND AVOCADO SALAD

DAIRY-FREE, GLUTEN-FREE, NUT-FREE

Servings: 2 / Prep time: 10 minutes

Since both shrimp and avocados don't stay fresh for long, this recipe only makes two servings. It will keep well in the fridge for up to three days. The acid in the orange and lime juice keeps the avocado from browning and adds lots of flavor to this delicious and quick salad.

Juice of 1 lime

Juice of ¼ orange

1 avocado, peeled, pitted, and cut into cubes

6 ounces cooked baby shrimp

¼ red onion, finely chopped

½ fennel bulb finely chopped

1 tablespoon chopped fennel fronds

¼ teaspoon sea salt

2 tablespoons mayonnaise or plain Greek yogurt

1. In a medium bowl, squeeze the lime juice and orange juice over the avocado and mix well.

2. Add the shrimp, red onion, fennel bulb, fennel fronds, and salt. Mix well.

3. Add the mayonnaise or Greek yogurt and mix well.

4. Spoon into two containers. Place plastic wrap directly on the surface of the salad and then put a lid on the container. Refrigerate.

**COOKING TIP:** Don't skip the step of squeezing the citrus juice directly on the avocado and mixing it or the step of putting plastic directly on the surface of the salad. Both of these serve to keep the avocado from browning as it rests.

Per Serving: Calories: 429; Total Fat: 31g; Saturated Fat: 4.5g; Cholesterol: 129mg; Carbohydrates: 24g; Fiber: 7.5g; Protein: 15g

# SLOW COOKER PORK CHILI COLORADO

DAIRY-FREE, GLUTEN-FREE, NUT-FREE

*Servings: 6 / Prep time: 10 minutes / Cook time: 8 hours*

This is a true southwestern chili with smoky flavors. It also has just a few ingredients, and it's so easy to make. You can jazz it up with chopped avocados and cheese as a garnish, or eat it exactly as it is. It will keep in the fridge for up to five days, and it freezes extremely well, so double batches are encouraged.

3 pounds pork shoulder, cut into 1-inch pieces

1 onion, chopped

2 tablespoons chili powder

1 teaspoon chipotle chili powder

¼ cup water or broth

¼ cup whiskey

1 teaspoon sea salt

1. Combine all ingredients in a slow cooker.

2. Cover and cook on low for 8 hours. Once cooking is complete, turn off slow cooker. Let cool.

3. Divide evenly between six containers and refrigerate.

> **SUBSTITUTION TIP:** If you're not a whiskey fan, you can omit that and replace it with an additional ¼ cup of broth or water.

Per Serving: Calories: 467; Total Fat: 28g; Saturated Fat: 9.5g; Cholesterol: 143mg; Carbohydrates: 2g; Fiber: 0.5g; Protein: 43g

# ASIAN-INSPIRED PORK WITH SPICY SLAW

DAIRY-FREE, GLUTEN-FREE, NUT-FREE

*Servings: 4 / Prep time: 10 minutes / Cook time: 20 minutes*

If you enjoy Asian flavor profiles, then you'll love this pork and spicy slaw. With flavors of ginger, cilantro, scallions, and lime as well as a strong kick from the vinaigrette for the slaw, it's a tasty lunch that will wake up your taste buds. It will also keep in the fridge for up to five days, and you can freeze the pork for up to six months.

¼ cup apple cider vinegar

Juice of 2 limes

1 teaspoon sriracha

3 garlic cloves, minced

1 teaspoon grated ginger root

½ teaspoon sea salt

1 teaspoon granulated sugar

½ teaspoon Chinese hot mustard

¼ cup olive oil

1 pork tenderloin (1 to 1½ pounds)

4 cups shredded cabbage or coleslaw mix

1 bunch scallions, sliced

4 radishes, julienned

¼ cup chopped fresh cilantro

1. In a bowl, whisk together the apple cider vinegar, lime juice, sriracha, garlic cloves, ginger, salt, sugar, Chinese hot mustard, and olive oil. Divide in half.

2. Pour half of the mixture into a zipper bag with the pork tenderloin. Marinate for 3 hours.

3. Preheat the oven to 350°F.

4. Roast the pork tenderloin on a rimmed baking sheet until it reaches an internal temperature of 145°F, about 20 minutes. Rest the pork while you prepare the slaw.

5. In a large bowl, combine the cabbage, scallions, radish, and cilantro. Divide mix evenly between four containers.

6. Whisk the remaining dressing and pour it over the slaw. Slice the pork and place it on top of the slaw. Cover containers and refrigerate.

> **INGREDIENT TIP:** Some people are genetically predisposed to disliking cilantro—it tastes like soap to them. If you have this genetic predisposition, it's perfectly fine to omit the cilantro.

Per Serving: Calories: 255; Total Fat: 12g; Saturated Fat: 2.5g; Cholesterol: 76mg; Carbohydrates: 7g; Fiber: 2.5g; Protein: 29g

# SAUSAGE MEATBALL HEROES
NUT-FREE

*Servings: 4 / Prep time: 10 minutes / Cook time: 25 minutes*

If you're looking for a hearty lunch, then this is the perfect meal for you. Prepare the meatballs and sauce and store them separately, spooning the filling into the rolls just before eating so they don't get soggy. Meatballs will store for up to five days in the fridge or six months in the freezer.

½ cup milk

½ cup bread crumbs

1 pound bulk Italian sausage

2 tablespoons dried Italian seasoning, divided

2 teaspoons garlic powder, divided

1 teaspoon sea salt, divided

2 tablespoons olive oil

1 onion, chopped

1 (15-ounce) can crushed tomatoes

Pinch red pepper flakes

4 hero rolls, sliced open

1. In a large bowl, combine the milk and bread crumbs. Rest for 10 minutes.

2. Add sausage, 1 tablespoon of Italian seasoning, 1 teaspoon of garlic powder, and ½ teaspoon of salt. Mix well and form into 1-inch meatballs.

3. In a large pot, heat the olive oil over medium-high heat until it shimmers. Cook the meatballs, turning, until cooked through, 7 to 10 minutes.

4. Remove the meatballs from the fat in the pan with tongs and set them aside. Add the onion to the pan. Cook, stirring, until soft, about 5 minutes.

5. Add the crushed tomatoes, the remaining 1 tablespoon of Italian seasoning, the remaining 1 teaspoon of garlic powder, the remaining ½ teaspoon of sea salt, and the red pepper flakes. Bring to a simmer, stirring occasionally, for 5 minutes.

6. Return the meatballs to the pan. Simmer for 3 minutes more. Cool and divide evenly between four containers. Refrigerate.

7. When ready to eat, spoon the meatballs and sauce onto the hero rolls.

Per Serving: Calories: 683; Total Fat: 26g; Saturated Fat: 6.5g; Cholesterol: 36mg; Carbohydrates: 84g; Fiber: 5.5g; Protein: 24g

# ITALIAN SAUSAGE AND CARAMELIZED ONION SOUP

DAIRY-FREE, GLUTEN-FREE, NUT-FREE

*Servings: 6 / Prep time: 10 minutes / Cook time: 40 minutes*

The deep flavors of caramelized onions and the savory sausage make this soup so satisfying. You can use either bulk Italian sausage or sliced Italian sausages—both work well. For a spicier soup, use hot Italian sausage. This will keep in the fridge for up to five days or in the freezer for up to six months.

2 tablespoons olive oil

1 pound Italian sausage

2 onions, thinly sliced

½ teaspoon sea salt

1 teaspoon dried thyme

½ cup dry white wine or dry sherry

6 cups low-sodium chicken broth

¼ teaspoon freshly cracked black pepper

1. In a large pot, heat olive oil over medium-high heat until it shimmers. Add the Italian sausage and cook, crumbling with a wooden spoon, until browned, about 5 minutes.

2. Remove the sausage from the fat in the pot with a slotted spoon and set it aside on a platter. Maintain the heat on the fat from the sausage and add the onions. Reduce the heat to medium-low.

3. Add the salt and thyme. Cook, stirring occasionally, until the onions are deeply browned, about 30 minutes.

4. Add the white wine or cooking sherry and use the side of the spoon to scrape any browned bits from the bottom of the pan.

5. Add the broth, pepper, and cooked sausage. Bring to a simmer. Cook for 5 minutes. Remove from heat and let cool.

6. Divide evenly between six containers and refrigerate.

> **SUBSTITUTION TIP:** If you don't want to add wine or sherry, then just use an additional ½ cup of broth.

Per Serving: Calories: 348; Total Fat: 28g; Saturated Fat: 9g; Cholesterol: 58mg; Carbohydrates: 5g; Fiber: 0.5g; Protein: 13g

Dried Fruit and Nut Dark
Chocolate Bark

*Page 141*

# Chapter 14
# SNACKS

# BANANA NUT MUFFINS

VEGETARIAN

*Servings: 12 / Prep time: 15 minutes / Cook time: 15 minutes*

If you've got browning bananas lying around, then it's time to make banana nut muffins. It's a great way to use up fruit you probably won't eat, and muffins are a meal prepper's dream because they keep well in the freezer for up to six months. Store these, tightly sealed, at room temperature, for up to five days.

½ cup unsalted butter, melted and cooled slightly

¾ cup brown sugar

2 eggs, beaten

2 teaspoons vanilla extract

3 very ripe bananas, peeled and mashed

1¾ cups all-purpose flour

1 teaspoon baking soda

½ teaspoon ground cinnamon

¼ teaspoon sea salt

½ cup chopped pecans

1. Preheat the oven to 350°F. Grease a twelve-cup muffin tin or line it with muffin liners.

2. In a large bowl, whisk together the butter and brown sugar until well blended.

3. Add the eggs and vanilla and whisk well.

4. Whisk in the bananas.

5. In another bowl, combine the flour, baking soda, cinnamon, and salt. Whisk to blend.

6. Pour the dry ingredients into the wet and fold until just combined. There will be streaks of flour that remain in the bowl. Gently fold in the pecans.

7. Spoon into the prepared muffin cups until each is about three-quarters full. Bake in the preheated oven until a toothpick inserted in the center of a muffin comes out clean, about 15 minutes. Cool on a wire rack. Store in a resealable bag.

> **SUBSTITUTION TIP:** It's easy to turn these into pumpkin muffins with a few simple substitutions. Replace the bananas with 2 cups of canned pumpkin puree (not pumpkin pie mix). Replace the cinnamon with 1 teaspoon of pumpkin pie spice.

Per Serving: (1 muffin) Calories: 258; Total Fat: 12g; Saturated Fat: 5g; Cholesterol: 51mg; Carbohydrates: 35g; Fiber: 1.5g; Protein: 4g

# HUMMUS DEVILED EGGS

DAIRY-FREE, GLUTEN-FREE, NUT-FREE, VEGETARIAN

*Servings: 6 / Prep time: 15 minutes*

Using hummus in place of mayonnaise lowers the fat and cholesterol in deviled eggs and adds an interesting flavor. You can use any store-bought hummus or make the Edamame Hummus with Jicama Sticks (page 134). These will keep in the fridge for about five days. Don't freeze.

6 hard-boiled eggs, peeled and halved lengthwise

½ cup store-bought hummus

¼ teaspoon sea salt

2 tablespoons chopped fresh Italian parsley

¼ cup chopped roasted red bell pepper

1. Using a teaspoon, scoop the yolks from the egg-white halves. Put the egg whites on a plate and the yolks in a bowl. Mash the yolks with a fork.

2. Add the hummus, salt, parsley, and red bell pepper. Mix well.

3. Spoon the mixture back into the egg halves. Divide evenly between six containers and refrigerate.

> **INGREDIENT TIP:** Want to add some texture? Stir in ¼ cup of pepitas or pine nuts to the hummus and yolk mixture.

Per Serving: (2 egg halves) Calories: 107; Total Fat: 6.5g; Saturated Fat: 2g; Cholesterol: 186mg; Carbohydrates: 4g; Fiber: 1g; Protein: 8g

# CHOCOLATE ZUCCHINI MUFFINS

NUT-FREE, VEGETARIAN

*Servings: 12 / Prep time: 15 minutes / Cook time: 25 minutes*

There comes a certain time every year when people who garden—and their friends and family—have a lot of zucchini. If you're working to figure out what to do with that zucchini, quick breads and muffins are always a great way to use it up. These muffins are moist and rich, and they freeze well for up to six months. You can also store them at room temperature for up to five days.

½ cup unsalted butter, melted and cooled slightly

¼ cup packed brown sugar

¾ cup granulated sugar

2 eggs

1 teaspoon vanilla extract

1¼ cups all-purpose flour

¼ cup unsweetened cocoa powder

½ teaspoon sea salt

½ teaspoon baking soda

½ teaspoon cinnamon

1 cup grated zucchini

1 cup chocolate chips

1. Preheat the oven to 350°F. Grease a twelve-cup muffin tin or line it with muffin liners.

2. In a large bowl, whisk together the butter, brown sugar, and sugar.

3. Whisk in the eggs and vanilla.

4. In another bowl, combine the flour, cocoa powder, salt, baking soda, and cinnamon.

5. Pour the dry ingredients into the wet and fold until just combined. There will be streaks of flour that remain in the bowl.

6. Fold in the zucchini and chocolate chips until just combined.

7. Spoon into the prepared muffin cups until each is about three-quarters full. Bake in the preheated oven until a toothpick inserted in the center of a muffin comes out clean, 15 to 20 minutes. Cool on a wire rack. Store in a resealable bag.

Per Serving: (1 muffin) Calories: 292; Total Fat: 17g; Saturated Fat: 9.5g; Cholesterol: 51mg; Carbohydrates: 39g; Fiber: 4g; Protein: 4g

# APPLE-CINNAMON GREEK YOGURT PARFAIT

GLUTEN-FREE, VEGETARIAN

*Servings: 4 / Prep time: 10 minutes / Cook time: 10 minutes*

Greek yogurt is nearly the perfect snack food because it's tangy and creamy, and it's packed with protein. It's also a super versatile ingredient because its neutral flavor profile pairs so well with so many ingredients. Here, it's paired with brown sugar, cinnamon, apples, and chopped walnuts for a really tasty treat.

2 tablespoons unsalted butter

3 apples, peeled, cored, and chopped

¼ cup packed brown sugar

1 teaspoon cinnamon

¼ cup apple cider

2 cups plain whole-milk Greek yogurt

½ cup chopped walnuts

1. In a large skillet, heat the butter over medium-high heat until it bubbles.

2. Add the apples and cook, stirring occasionally, until they begin to soften, about 5 minutes.

3. Add the brown sugar, cinnamon, and apple cider. Cook, stirring, until the sugar is dissolved, and the syrup thickens, about 5 minutes more. Cool completely.

4. In four containers, layer the yogurt, apples, and walnuts. Store in the fridge for up to 5 days.

> **INGREDIENT TIP:** Sweet-tart apples are your best bet here. Try Granny Smith, Braeburn, or Pink Lady varieties, which all have a nice sweet-tart flavor that holds up to the brown sugar and cinnamon.

Per Serving: Calories: 401; Total Fat: 22g; Saturated Fat: 7.5g; Cholesterol: 32mg; Carbohydrates: 41g; Fiber: 4.5g; Protein: 14g

# EDAMAME HUMMUS WITH JICAMA STICKS

DAIRY-FREE, GLUTEN-FREE, NUT-FREE, VEGAN

*Servings: 4 / Prep time: 10 minutes / Cook time: 10 minutes*

Pretty much any starchy legume can be made into a soft, smooth puree, and edamame is no exception. These fresh soybeans are high in both protein and starch, and they have a bright green color that makes this a colorful snack. Here, it's paired with jicama, but feel free to use any chopped or sliced veggies for a delicious dipper. This will keep in the fridge for up to five days. It won't freeze well.

1¼ cups fresh or frozen (thawed) shelled edamame

¼ cup tahini

¼ cup lemon juice

1 garlic clove, finely minced

2 tablespoons olive oil

¼ cup chopped fresh Italian parsley

½ teaspoon sea salt

1 bulb of jicama, peeled and julienned

1. In a blender or food processor, combine the edamame, tahini, lemon juice, garlic, olive oil, parsley, and salt. Blend until smooth.

2. Divide evenly between four containers and refrigerate. Serve with the jicama for dipping.

> **COOKING TIP:** It's super easy to change up the flavors in hummus. By changing the legume you use, in a 1:1 substitution or adding ingredients such as roasted red peppers in place of the parsley in a 1:1 substitution, you can create your own flavor of hummus.

Per Serving: Calories: 278; Total Fat: 17g; Saturated Fat: 2g; Cholesterol: 0mg; Carbohydrates: 25g; Fiber: 11g; Protein: 9g

# PB AND JELLY GREEK YOGURT JARS

GLUTEN-FREE, VEGETARIAN

*Servings: 2 / Prep time: 5 minutes*

These Greek yogurt jars are super simple, and they'll make you feel like a kid again. If you have homemade jam or jelly, by all means, use it. Otherwise, choose your favorite flavor of low-sugar or no-sugar fruit preserves and sugar-free natural peanut butter for an adult upgrade on a childhood favorite. It will keep in the fridge for up to five days.

1 cup plain whole-milk Greek yogurt

¼ cup natural peanut butter

¼ cup low-sugar fruit preserves

1. Spoon the yogurt into two small mason jars.

2. Drizzle with the peanut butter and spoon the preserves over the top. Refrigerate.

**SUBSTITUTION TIP:** If you were more of a peanut butter and banana kid, then replace the fruit preserves with sliced bananas. If you're allergic to peanuts, substitute almond butter.

Per Serving: Calories: 403; Total Fat: 22g; Saturated Fat: 5.5g; Cholesterol: 17mg; Carbohydrates: 29g; Fiber: 2g; Protein: 18g

# HONEY AND ORANGE CORN MUFFINS

NUT-FREE, VEGETARIAN

*Servings: 12 / Prep time: 5 minutes / Cook time: 15 minutes*

Corn muffins are little yellow pillows of delight, especially when they're scented with orange and sweetened with honey. They also freeze well—for up to six months—and, properly stored, they'll keep on the counter for about five days.

¼ cup unsalted butter, melted and cooled slightly

½ cup milk

½ cup freshly squeezed orange juice

⅓ cup honey

1 large egg

1 cup cornmeal

1 cup all-purpose flour

3 teaspoons baking soda

Grated zest from 1 orange

¼ teaspoon sea salt

1. Preheat the oven to 425°F. Grease a twelve-cup muffin tin or add muffin liners.

2. In a large bowl, whisk together the butter, milk, orange juice, honey, and egg.

3. In another bowl, whisk together the cornmeal, flour, baking soda, orange zest, and salt.

4. Add the dry ingredients to the wet and stir until just combined.

5. Spoon into the muffin cups, filling each about three-quarters full. Bake in the preheated oven until a toothpick inserted in the center comes out clean, about 15 minutes. Cool on a wire rack. Store in a resealable bag or container.

> **COOKING TIP:** Add a tasty surprise in the center of your corn muffins. Fill the muffin cup about half full and add ½ teaspoon of orange marmalade or cranberry jelly. Finish filling the cup and bake as written.

Per Serving: (1 muffin) Calories: 165; Total Fat: 5g; Saturated Fat: 2.5g; Cholesterol: 27mg; Carbohydrates: 27g; Fiber: 1g; Protein: 3g

# CORN AND BEAN SALSA WITH CHIPS

DAIRY-FREE, NUT-FREE, VEGAN

*Servings: 6 / Prep time: 5 minutes*

Fresh salsa is so easy to make. It's especially delicious when corn and/or tomatoes are in season, so use as many fresh, local veggies in this as possible for the best flavor. It will store well in the fridge for about five days. It's also delicious with some of the recipes in this book such as the Chile-Lime Shrimp Fajitas (page 121) or the Chicken and Black Bean Taco Salad (page 108). For breakfast, spoon it onto your cooked eggs.

1 cup corn (fresh, frozen, or canned)

1 (15-ounce) can black beans, drained

2 large tomatoes, chopped

½ red onion, finely chopped

1 jalapeño, seeded and minced

1 garlic clove, chopped

¼ cup chopped fresh cilantro

Juice of 1 lime

½ teaspoon sea salt

6 cups tortilla chips

1. In a medium bowl, combine the corn, black beans, tomatoes, red onion, jalapeño, garlic, cilantro, lime juice, and salt. Mix well.

2. Divide the salsa evenly between six containers. Serve with chips for dipping.

> **SUBSTITUTION TIP:** Other fruits make a great substitute for tomatoes to change the flavors of the salsa. Watermelon, cantaloupe, and mango all work well here. Replace the tomatoes with 1 cup of chopped fruit.

137

Per Serving: Calories: 244; Total Fat: 8g; Saturated Fat: 1g; Cholesterol: 0mg; Carbohydrates: 37g; Fiber: 6g; Protein: 7.5g

# TURKEY ROLL-UPS

GLUTEN-FREE, NUT-FREE

*Servings: 4 / Prep time: 10 minutes / Cook time: 5 minutes*

This is probably one of the simplest recipes in this entire cookbook, but it's very versatile (change to add your own favorite ingredients), and it's super tasty. If you can find it, opt for low-sodium deli turkey. Blanching the asparagus keeps it bright green, and it tenderizes the asparagus without making it too soft. This will keep in the fridge for five days.

1 teaspoon sea salt

1 bunch of
  asparagus, trimmed

½ cup softened cream cheese

1 teaspoon Dijon mustard

1 tablespoon chopped
  fresh chives

1 tablespoon chopped
  fresh dill

12 slices deli turkey

1. In a large pot, bring a large quantity of water and the salt to a boil. (There should be enough water to cover the asparagus by an inch.)

2. Add the asparagus and cover. Cook for 3 minutes.

3. Drain in a colander and run under cold water to stop the cooking. Cool.

4. In a small bowl, mix the cream cheese, mustard, chives, and dill.

5. Spread cream cheese mixture on each slice of turkey. Place a piece of asparagus on the cream cheese mixture and roll.

6. Divide evenly between four containers and refrigerate.

---

**SUBSTITUTION TIP:** Save time by using an herbed cheese, such as Boursin, in place of the cream cheese, mustard, chives, and dill.

---

Per Serving: (3 roll-ups) Calories: 157; Total Fat: 11g; Saturated Fat: 6g; Cholesterol: 50mg; Carbohydrates: 5g; Fiber: 1g; Protein: 10g

# CUCUMBER SMOKED SALMON ROLLS

DAIRY-FREE, GLUTEN-FREE, NUT-FREE

*Servings: 4 / Prep time: 15 minutes*

This is another very easy recipe, and it doesn't involve any cooking at all. Because it contains smoked salmon, it will keep well in the fridge for about five days, and its smoky and rich flavors are cut with the crisp acidity of the cucumbers.

6 ounces smoked salmon, chopped

Grated zest of 1 lemon

1 tablespoon chopped fresh dill

3 radishes, grated

¼ cup mayonnaise

1 cucumber, cut into long ribbons with a vegetable peeler

1. In a small bowl, combine the smoked salmon, lemon zest, dill, radishes, and mayonnaise.

2. Spread on the cucumber ribbons and roll into rolls.

3. Divide evenly between four containers and refrigerate.

> **SUBSTITUTION TIP:** You can also do this with 6 ounces of canned tuna, drained.

Per Serving: Calories: 151; Total Fat: 12g; Saturated Fat: 2g; Cholesterol: 16mg; Carbohydrates: 3g; Fiber: 1g; Protein: 9g

# BAKED JALAPEÑO POPPERS

GLUTEN-FREE, NUT-FREE, VEGETARIAN

*Servings: 6 / Prep time: 15 minutes / Cook time: 10 minutes*

Whether you like to eat them plain or you prefer to dip them in salsa, guacamole, sour cream, or pepper jelly, jalapeño poppers are the perfect bite-size snack. This version makes them healthier than traditional poppers, which are fried. Make sure you soften the cream cheese, so it blends and spreads easily. Keep these in the fridge for up to five days or in the freezer for up to six months.

8 ounces cream cheese, softened

Grated zest of 1 lime

1 garlic clove, minced

¼ cup finely minced scallions

¼ cup chopped fresh cilantro

12 large jalapeño peppers, halved lengthwise with ribs and seeds removed

½ cup shredded Pepper Jack cheese

1. Preheat the oven to 425°F.

2. In a food processor or blender, combine the cream cheese, lime zest, garlic, scallions, and cilantro. Pulse in 1-second pulses 10 to 20 times until well blended.

3. Place the jalapeño peppers on a rimmed baking sheet and fill each with the cream cheese mixture.

4. Sprinkle with the Pepper Jack cheese.

5. Bake in the preheated oven until bubbly, about 12 minutes. Remove from oven and let cool.

6. Divide evenly between six containers and refrigerate.

> **DIETARY SWAP:** To include animal protein, add up to ½ cup of crab or baby shrimp. Fold it into the cream cheese mixture.

Per Serving: (2 jalapeño poppers) Calories: 176; Total Fat: 16g; Saturated Fat: 9.5g; Cholesterol: 47mg; Carbohydrates: 5g; Fiber: 1g; Protein: 5g

# DRIED FRUIT AND NUT DARK CHOCOLATE BARK

GLUTEN-FREE, VEGETARIAN

*Servings: 24 / Prep time: 15 minutes / Cook time: 10 minutes*

This recipe makes a lot of servings, but it freezes well, so it's the perfect sometimes treat. It will keep in the freezer for up to 6 months or at room temperature for up to one week. It's also easy to vary by using your own choice of nuts and dried fruits.

12 ounces bittersweet chocolate, chopped

¾ cup chopped almonds

¼ cup dried cherries

Sprinkle of sea salt

1.  Melt the chocolate on a double boiler, stirring, until smooth.

2.  Cover a large, rimmed baking sheet with parchment paper. Spread the melted chocolate in an even layer on the sheet.

3.  Sprinkle with the almonds, cherries, and salt. Cool at room temperature until hard.

4.  Break into 24 pieces. Portion out into sandwich bags or reusable containers. Refrigerate or store in a cool, dry place.

> **SUBSTITUTION TIP:** Some combinations of fruit and nuts to try include dried apricots and chopped hazelnuts, dried cranberries and walnuts, and dried apples and pecans.

Per Serving: Calories: 93; Total Fat: 6.5g; Saturated Fat: 3g; Cholesterol: 0mg; Carbohydrates: 9g; Fiber: 2g; Protein: 1g

Ranch Dressing

Page 145

## Chapter 15
# DRESSINGS AND SAUCES

# GREEK YOGURT DRESSING

GLUTEN-FREE, NUT-FREE, VEGETARIAN

*Servings: 6 / Prep time: 10 minutes*

This blender dressing is fast and easy, and it has lots of fresh herb flavor that makes it a satisfying salad dressing, tasty on seafood, poultry, or meat, or delicious as a dip for veggies. It's high in protein from the Greek yogurt, and it has a distinctive tang. It will keep in the fridge for up to one week.

¼ cup chopped fresh basil

¼ cup chopped fresh Italian parsley

2 garlic cloves, minced

¼ cup chopped, roasted red bell peppers

¼ cup plain whole-milk Greek yogurt

1 teaspoon Dijon mustard

Grated zest and juice of 1 lemon

½ teaspoon sea salt

¼ teaspoon freshly cracked black pepper

1. In a blender or food processor, combine the basil, parsley, garlic, and bell peppers. Pulse in 1-second pulses 20 times to chop all ingredients.

2. Add the yogurt, mustard, lemon zest and juice, salt, and pepper. Blend until smooth.

3. Store in an airtight container and refrigerate.

> **DIETARY SWAP:** Make this dairy-free by substituting any plain nondairy yogurt for the Greek yogurt and adding a tablespoon or two of nondairy milk to adjust the consistency.

Per Serving: Calories: 18; Total Fat: 0.5g; Saturated Fat: 0.5g; Cholesterol: 1mg; Carbohydrates: 2g; Fiber: 0g; Protein: 1g

# RANCH DRESSING

GLUTEN-FREE, NUT-FREE, VEGETARIAN

*Servings: 6 / Prep time: 10 minutes*

Are you a ranch dressing fan? Making it yourself with fresh herbs is a revelation—it's so vibrant and fresh tasting in a way that bottled dressing will never be. It will store in the fridge for up to one week.

2 tablespoons mayonnaise

2 tablespoons buttermilk

2 tablespoons sour cream

1 tablespoon chopped
   fresh dill

1 tablespoon chopped
   fresh parsley

1 tablespoon chopped
   fresh chives

1 garlic clove, minced

¼ teaspoon onion powder

⅛ teaspoon sea salt

⅛ teaspoon black pepper

Grated zest and juice
   of 1 lemon

1. In a bowl, whisk together the mayonnaise, buttermilk, and sour cream.

2. Stir in the dill, parsley, chives, garlic, onion powder, salt, pepper, and lemon zest and juice.

3. Store in an airtight container and refrigerate.

> **COOKING TIP:** While this doesn't freeze well, it definitely doubles or triples easily if you're cooking for a crowd and want to add fresh dressing.

Per Serving: Calories: 48; Total Fat: 4.5g; Saturated Fat: 1g; Cholesterol: 6mg; Carbohydrates: 2g; Fiber: 0g; Protein: 1g

# COBB SALAD DRESSING

DAIRY-FREE, GLUTEN-FREE, NUT-FREE, VEGAN

*Servings: 6 / Prep time: 10 minutes*

Cobb salad dressing is a delicious, light vinaigrette that complements the other flavors found in Cobb salads (see Chicken and Corn Cobb Salad on page 93). It's also delicious on other salads or even as a marinade for poultry or fish. This will keep in the fridge for about two weeks, so you can make a larger batch, as well. Don't freeze it.

1 tablespoon red wine vinegar

Juice of 1 lemon

2 garlic cloves, minced

1 teaspoon Dijon mustard

1 teaspoon granulated sugar

¼ teaspoon sea salt

⅛ teaspoon freshly cracked black pepper

¼ cup olive oil

1. Whisk together in a bowl the vinegar, lemon juice, garlic, mustard, sugar, sea salt, pepper, and oil.

2. Store in an airtight container and refrigerate.

> **COOKING TIP:** Feel free to add chopped or dried herbs, such as oregano, to flavor your dressing.

Per Serving: Calories: 87; Total Fat: 9g; Saturated Fat: 1g; Cholesterol: 0mg; Carbohydrates: 2g; Fiber: 0g; Protein: 0g

146

# SWEET AND SPICY BARBECUE SAUCE

DAIRY-FREE, GLUTEN-FREE, NUT-FREE, VEGAN

*Servings: 12 / Prep time: 10 minutes / Cook time: 10 minutes*

The trick to making barbecue sauce taste like barbecue sauce is the use of liquid smoke. With liquid smoke, a very little goes a long way, but it adds that smoky flavor that makes barbecue sauce so delicious. This sauce will store for about two weeks in the fridge.

1 tablespoon olive oil

1 shallot, peeled and minced

1 cup tomato sauce

¼ cup apple cider vinegar

¼ cup dark brown sugar

½ teaspoon liquid smoke

1 teaspoon garlic powder

1 teaspoon onion powder

½ teaspoon sea salt

¼ teaspoon cayenne (or to taste)

1. In a medium pot, heat the olive oil over medium-high heat until it shimmers.

2. Add the shallot and cook, stirring, until soft, about 3 minutes.

3. Add the tomato sauce, apple cider vinegar, brown sugar, liquid smoke, garlic powder, onion powder, salt, and cayenne. Cook, stirring, until the sauce thickens, about 5 minutes. Remove from heat and let cool.

4. Store in an airtight container and refrigerate.

> **COOKING TIP:** You can also use fresh garlic in place of the garlic powder. Omit the garlic powder. Instead, in step 2, add 2 minced garlic cloves with the shallots.

Per Serving: Calories: 35; Total Fat: 1g; Saturated Fat: 0g; Cholesterol: 0mg; Carbohydrates: 6g; Fiber: 0.5g; Protein: 0g

147

# EASY PEANUT SAUCE

DAIRY-FREE, VEGAN

*Servings: 6 / Prep time: 10 minutes*

Whether you want your peanut sauce for dipping or drizzling on meat, or you like it on noodles as a meal by itself, this quick and easy sauce is super satisfying. Mix it in a single step in the blender or food processor and store it in the fridge for up to two weeks.

¼ cup natural peanut butter

1 tablespoon low-sodium soy sauce

1 garlic clove, minced

1 teaspoon grated ginger root

½ teaspoon sriracha

Juice of 1 lime

Water to adjust texture

1. Combine all ingredients in a blender or food processor and blend until smooth. If the sauce is too thick, add water 1 tablespoon at a time until reaching the right consistency.

2. Store in an airtight container and refrigerate.

> **SUBSTITUTION TIP:** Make this gluten-free by replacing the soy sauce with gluten-free tamari.

Per Serving: Calories: 74; Total Fat: 5.5g; Saturated Fat: 1g; Cholesterol: 0mg; Carbohydrates: 3g; Fiber: 0.5g; Protein: 3g

# GUACAMOLE

DAIRY-FREE, GLUTEN-FREE, NUT-FREE, VEGAN

*Servings: 6 / Prep time: 10 minutes*

Guacamole is a favorite Tex-Mex classic, and it's easy to see why. It's creamy and delicious with a nice acidity as well. It also browns very easily, so to keep the avocado from browning, store it in the fridge with plastic wrap directly on the surface to keep air from getting to it. It will store for up to four days.

Juice of 1 lime

2 soft avocados, peeled, pitted, and cubed

¼ red onion, finely chopped

1 garlic clove, minced

2 tablespoons chopped fresh cilantro

½ teaspoon sea salt

1. In a medium bowl, squeeze the lime juice over the avocado pieces.

2. Add the red onion, garlic, cilantro, and salt. Mash with a fork.

3. Store in an airtight container and refrigerate.

> **INGREDIENT TIP:** Always use fresh lemon or lime juice (you'll need about 2 tablespoons of juice altogether), which has the best flavor for guacamole.

Per Serving: Calories: 80; Total Fat: 7g; Saturated Fat: 1g; Cholesterol: 0mg; Carbohydrates: 5g; Fiber: 3g; Protein: 1g

# CILANTRO-LIME DRESSING

DAIRY-FREE, GLUTEN-FREE, NUT-FREE, VEGAN

*Servings: 6 / Prep time: 10 minutes*

Lime and cilantro are a classic flavor combination for southwestern and Asian foods. This version has a southwestern flair, with a hint of garlic and a pinch of cayenne as well. It makes a great marinade for fish or poultry, and it's mighty good on a salad as well.

¼ cup olive oil

Grated zest and juice
  of 1 lime

1 garlic clove, minced

¼ teaspoon mustard powder

¼ cup chopped fresh cilantro

½ teaspoon sea salt

Pinch cayenne

1. In a medium bowl, whisk together the oil, lime zest and juice, garlic, mustard powder, cilantro, salt, and cayenne until combined.

2. Store in an airtight container and refrigerate.

> **SUBSTITUTION TIP:** It's easy to vary this basic vinaigrette recipe by replacing the lime juice (which is about 2 tablespoons) with an equal amount of another acid such as lemon juice or vinegar and replacing the herbs with equal amounts of other herbs, such as basil. Don't omit the mustard powder, as it serves as an emulsifier to keep the fat and acid mixed.

Per Serving: Calories: 82; Total Fat: 9g; Saturated Fat: 1g; Cholesterol: 0mg; Carbohydrates: 1g; Fiber: 0g; Protein: 0g

# HONEY MUSTARD DRESSING

DAIRY-FREE, GLUTEN-FREE, NUT-FREE, VEGETARIAN

*Servings: 6 / Prep time: 10 minutes*

Another classic dressing, honey mustard is sweet and savory all at once. This simple recipe uses Dijon mustard, which is often gluten-free, and apple cider vinegar, which has a distinct tang. It will store in the fridge for up to two weeks.

2 tablespoons Dijon mustard

2 tablespoons honey

2 tablespoons apple cider vinegar

½ teaspoon sea salt

¼ cup olive oil

1. In a medium bowl, whisk together the mustard, honey, vinegar, salt, and oil until combined.

2. Store in an airtight container and refrigerate.

> **SUBSTITUTION TIP:** Feel free to add 1 tablespoon of finely minced shallot for additional flavor.

Per Serving: Calories: 107; Total Fat: 9g; Saturated Fat: 1g; Cholesterol: 0mg; Carbohydrates: 6g; Fiber: 0g; Protein: 0g

# LEMON-DIJON VINAIGRETTE

DAIRY-FREE, GLUTEN-FREE, NUT-FREE, VEGAN

*Servings: 6 / Prep time: 10 minutes*

The brightness of lemon blends beautifully with Dijon mustard, while shallots and garlic add additional depth. Try this on a piece of whitefish, as a marinade for chicken breast, or topping your favorite salad.

¼ cup olive oil

Grated zest and juice of 1 lemon

1 tablespoon Dijon mustard

1 tablespoon finely minced shallot

1 garlic clove, minced

¼ teaspoon sea salt

1. In a medium bowl, whisk together the oil, lemon zest and juice, mustard, shallot, garlic, and salt until combined.

2. Store in an airtight container and refrigerate.

**SUBSTITUTION TIP:** Turn this into an orange-tarragon dressing. You'll need the grated zest and juice from ½ an orange in place of the grated lemon zest and juice. Omit the garlic and add 1 tablespoon of chopped fresh tarragon or 1 teaspoon of dried tarragon.

Per Serving: Calories: 86; Total Fat: 9g; Saturated Fat: 1g; Cholesterol: 0mg; Carbohydrates: 1g; Fiber: 0g; Protein: 0g

# TZATZIKI

GLUTEN-FREE, NUT-FREE, VEGETARIAN

*Servings: 6 / Prep time: 10 minutes*

Tzatziki is a Greek yogurt-and-cucumber sauce that's super refreshing with food such as lamb. It's also a tasty dip for veggies or pita wedges, or even a yummy salad dressing. It doesn't freeze well, but will keep in the fridge for about five days.

½ cup plain whole-milk Greek yogurt

1 cucumber, grated

1 garlic clove, minced

½ teaspoon dried dill

1 tablespoon olive oil

Juice of ½ lemon

½ teaspoon sea salt

⅛ teaspoon pepper

1. In a medium bowl, whisk together the yogurt, cucumber, garlic, dill, oil, lemon juice, salt, and pepper until combined.

2. Store in an airtight container and refrigerate.

> **DIETARY SWAP:** Make this dairy-free and vegan by substituting a vegan yogurt, such as plain almond milk yogurt.

Per Serving: Calories: 46; Total Fat: 3.5g; Saturated Fat: 1g; Cholesterol: 3mg; Carbohydrates: 2g; Fiber: 0g; Protein: 2g

153

# LEMON-GARLIC SAUCE

DAIRY-FREE, GLUTEN-FREE, NUT-FREE, VEGAN

*Servings: 6 / Prep time: 10 minutes*

Fair warning—this sauce is super garlicky. It's also addictive. It's a version of garlic sauce, which is a traditional Lebanese sauce, and you can use it on poultry, fish, or meat, as well as with vegetables or even on your eggs for breakfast. This will store in the fridge for up to two weeks.

10 garlic cloves, minced

¼ cup freshly squeezed
  lemon juice

½ cup olive oil

½ teaspoon sea salt

1. Combine the garlic, lemon juice, oil, and salt in a blender or food processor and blend for 2 to 3 minutes, until thick and smooth.

2. Store in an airtight container and refrigerate.

Per Serving: Calories: 169; Total Fat: 18g; Saturated Fat: 2.5g; Cholesterol: 0mg; Carbohydrates: 2g; Fiber: 0g; Protein: 0g

# CHIPOTLE MAYO SAUCE

DAIRY-FREE, GLUTEN-FREE, NUT-FREE, VEGETARIAN

*Servings: 4 / Prep time: 10 minutes*

Whether you want this on a sandwich or burger or to drizzle on a salad, this smoky, spicy mayo is a surefire way to jazz up your food. You'll need to get chipotle chiles in adobo sauce, which you can find in the Mexican food section of the grocery store. It will keep for about a week in the fridge.

¼ cup mayonnaise

1 chipotle chile (from canned chipotle in adobo), minced

1 teaspoon adobo sauce reserved from the canned chiles

1. Combine the mayonnaise, chipotle chile, and adobo sauce in a blender or food processor and blend until smooth.

2. Store in an airtight container and refrigerate.

> **SUBSTITUTION TIP:** Make this vegan by using vegan mayo. You can also lower the fat content by replacing the mayonnaise with an equal amount of nonfat, plain Greek yogurt.

Per Serving: Calories: 96; Total Fat: 10g; Saturated Fat: 1.5g; Cholesterol: 6mg; Carbohydrates: 0g; Fiber: 0g; Protein: 0g

155

# MEASUREMENT CONVERSIONS

## VOLUME EQUIVALENTS (LIQUID)

| US Standard | US Standard (ounces) | Metric (approximate) |
| --- | --- | --- |
| 2 tablespoons | 1 fl. oz. | 30 mL |
| ¼ cup | 2 fl. oz. | 60 mL |
| ½ cup | 4 fl. oz. | 120 mL |
| 1 cup | 8 fl. oz. | 240 mL |
| 1½ cups | 12 fl. oz. | 355 mL |
| 2 cups or 1 pint | 16 fl. oz. | 475 mL |
| 4 cups or 1 quart | 32 fl. oz. | 1 L |
| 1 gallon | 128 fl. oz. | 4 L |

## OVEN TEMPERATURES

| Fahrenheit (F) | Celsius (C) (approximate) |
| --- | --- |
| 250°F | 120°C |
| 300°F | 150°C |
| 325°F | 165°C |
| 350°F | 180°C |
| 375°F | 190°C |
| 400°F | 200°C |
| 425°F | 220°C |
| 450°F | 230°C |

## VOLUME EQUIVALENTS (DRY)

| US Standard | Metric (approximate) |
| --- | --- |
| ⅛ teaspoon | 0.5 mL |
| ¼ teaspoon | 1 mL |
| ½ teaspoon | 2 mL |
| ¾ teaspoon | 4 mL |
| 1 teaspoon | 5 mL |
| 1 tablespoon | 15 mL |
| ¼ cup | 59 mL |
| ⅓ cup | 79 mL |
| ½ cup | 118 mL |
| ⅔ cup | 156 mL |
| ¾ cup | 177 mL |
| 1 cup | 235 mL |
| 2 cups or 1 pint | 475 mL |
| 3 cups | 700 mL |
| 4 cups or 1 quart | 1 L |

## WEIGHT EQUIVALENTS

| US Standard | Metric (approximate) |
| --- | --- |
| ½ ounce | 15 g |
| 1 ounce | 30 g |
| 2 ounces | 60 g |
| 4 ounces | 115 g |
| 8 ounces | 225 g |
| 12 ounces | 340 g |
| 16 ounces or 1 pound | 455 g |

# INDEX

**159**

**163**

167

168

169

# ACKNOWLEDGMENTS

Dear Jamie,

When I began writing this book, I didn't realize that life takes us on some crazy turns, and that our paths might diverge for a while. By the time this book is printed, I will be forging my road here on earth alone, and speaking to you in abstract terms, running my thoughts and decisions by you virtually.

I know many of us that were left behind will have to do the same. Every night before I go to sleep I look at the sign you got me, that promised you would love me for the rest of your life, even though you couldn't promise me you would be there for the rest of mine.

Maybe you knew more than I did, but either way, I need to thank you for the three amazing years that you gifted me as a husband and partner, and the 50 short, but incredible years, you gave everyone in your life as a father, friend, partner, son, and human being. You will be missed by the second, minute, hour, day, and lifetime that we remain here without you by our side.

I also want to express my deep gratitude to the community that was drawn to you throughout your life, and the life that we were building together. I wouldn't have been able to fulfill our dream if it had not been for the support and confidence instilled in me by our team, our gym members, the local residents in Almonte (the friendly town), our friends, our neighbors, our family, and our online community, who showed up day in and day out to make sure our gym would survive and that I was taken care of.

Finally, I need to thank my publisher, Callisto Media, for being so unbelievably patient and accommodating with me and making sure that this project could still be realized during such a difficult time, even though I was a bit of a mess. You have made this entire process seamless, and I am honored to have been able to be one of your authors. Thank you all.

In closing, life is hard and sweet, all at the same time. Until we meet again, I love you Jamie, and I know I will see you on the flip side.

As always, I love you more,
Michelle

# ABOUT THE AUTHOR

**Michelle Vodrazka** is the author of the best-selling book *Help Yourself to Seconds*, the e-book *Smart Snacking for Sports*, and *The Bodybuilding Meal Prep Cookbook*. She is a sought-after nutrition and fitness expert, blogger, international speaker, and corporate wellness consultant. She loves to share her knowledge of cooking, nutrition, and fitness on her website and with audiences nationwide.

Michelle has worked in the health and fitness field since she was 18 years old and has gathered numerous certifications along the way. These include certifications as a culinary nutrition expert, transformational nutrition coach, sports nutritionist, certified plant-based chef, yoga instructor, and personal trainer.

Michelle discovered her love for sports at the early age of four. She participated in gymnastics at the national level growing up, then fell in love with the gym culture in her early twenties and went on to compete in bodybuilding at the national level. Michelle has used her education and personal experience to help hundreds of other clients reach their own health and fitness goals.

Michelle lives in Ottawa, Canada, with her family, where she loves spending time exploring the outdoors and dreaming up new creations in her kitchen. You can connect with Michelle on social media on Facebook, Instagram, and on her website, MichelleVodrazka.com, where she shares her knowledge of cooking, nutrition, and fitness.

Printed in the USA
CPSIA information can be obtained
at www.ICGtesting.com
LVHW082042040124
767685LV00004B/23

9 781646 116614